ISBN 978-1-331-97317-1
PIBN 10262618

This book is a reproduction of an important historical work. Forgotten Books uses state-of-the-art technology to digitally reconstruct the work, preserving the original format whilst repairing imperfections present in the aged copy. In rare cases, an imperfection in the original, such as a blemish or missing page, may be replicated in our edition. We do, however, repair the vast majority of imperfections successfully; any imperfections that remain are intentionally left to preserve the state of such historical works.

Similar Books Are Available from
www.forgottenbooks.com

How to Teach Reading and Composition

BY

J. J. BURNS, M. A., Ph.D.

AUTHOR OF "THE STORY OF SHAKESPEARE'S ENGLISH KINGS."

———————

NEW YORK ·:· CINCINNATI ·:· CHICAGO

AMERICAN BOOK COMPANY

PREFACE.

THE purpose in the mind of the writer and compiler of this little book is to produce something which will help the teacher to prepare for the daily work of the schoolroom, at least the very important part of it embraced in the long labor of training boys and girls to read and to write the English language.

In his opinion, the results in these twin lines of educational work are not at all equal to those in some other lines much less important than these.

Judging from his experience and observation as a teacher and supervisor of reading classes, and trusting also to the judgment of teachers who have knowledge of the mode of presenting the subject as here given, the author believes that these discussions and lessons will be helpful. While they indicate methods, they do so by treating a number of pieces of literature either commonly found in books for reading, or eminently worthy of a place therein.

He asks of his readers a little patience, while he examines the results of the time expended on reading and composition in our elementary schools; he has made bold to point out defects and to suggest what seem to be remedies.

The subject of rhythm has been allowed space, as it is so generally overlooked, even by teachers of reading, and as it is an absolutely essential part of reading, prose as well as poetry.

It is claimed that there are two language exercises to which all others are subordinate : first, the guiding of pupils to get knowledge and culture from a book ; and, second, the training of pupils to express what they may know, or feel, with clearness and at least an approach to grace.

In the part of the book occupied by lessons for study, the easiest are at the beginning, and the most difficult are toward the end, but no special pains has been taken to make sure that each selection is easier than the one which follows it; nor are they all made use of after the same plan. To some, notes are appended ; of others, questions are asked ; sometimes both modes are used ; occasionally a passage akin to the one under the eye is quoted from some other writer, and this may be done simply to show the fuller content of a word. These quotations are, as a rule, of the finest, and deserve loving study.

The whole aim of the book is to set a proper example of reaching after the thought, to make clear the conviction that there is something there for the intellect and the emotions to feed upon, and that reading is a search for this.

Thanks are due to Messrs. Houghton, Mifflin & Co. for the privilege of using selections from Longfellow and Lowell.

CONTENTS.

PART I.—THE TEACHING OF ENGLISH IN ELEMENTARY SCHOOLS.

PART II.—SELECTED LESSONS FOR STUDY.

8   CONTENTS

PART I.

THE TEACHING OF ENGLISH IN ELEMENTARY SCHOOLS.

I. PRESENT METHODS AND THEIR RESULTS.

PUPILS, in high schools and colleges, taking what is called the classic course, study Latin. They learn the paradigms of inflected parts of speech, and the most common meanings of a variable number of words ; the rules of syntax are fixed in mind by endless repetition, and after a while those of prosody are encountered.

These young people would run a great risk should they, at a distance from the dictionary, attempt to render aloud a paragraph into their mother English ; and when they scan the lines of Vergil an attentive ear may catch the working of the machinery, the clicking of memory's valves, rather than the melody of the rhythm.

They learn, incidentally for the most part, to spell many of the words they use ; they transplant a few hundred roots that will perhaps bring forth fruit in their English vocabulary, but only in rare instances do they gain any power of thinking in Latin. This failure may be borne, however, if they are learning to think in their native speech.

9

Our boys and girls in all grades at school study English. They learn at great cost how to spell, upon special invitation, some hundreds of words; the ear, the eye, and the fingers being the weapons of this warfare. They learn some of the meanings of many of these words, while in various ways they acquire for use in oral speech a number of words a knowledge of whose spelling they have had no chance to gain.

They can open a book, and, with a greater or less degree of accuracy, follow lines of thought expressed by a writer who uses words with which they are familiar, or new ones whose meaning may be caught from the context, or selected from among the various definitions presented in a dictionary.

They acquire some familiarity with the paradigms of our common irregular words, with the rules of syntax which have been drawn up from an examination of the English sentence in all its forms, and which, once in a while, guide the learner in an attempt to construct sentences of the same fashion. However, when they speak or write correctly, their obedience to rule is likely to be for the most part unconscious,—"their's not to reason why," just then.

They catch the secret of those strange structures called diagrams, and, while I am not denying the value of this exercise, I am convinced that pupils often, and occasionally their teachers, think of the diagram as an end in itself. A diagram strips from a sentence all the thought and emotion that the author intended to convey therein, and although an understanding of these sentiments is more essential to literature than to grammar, it is highly important, of course, that the pupil should comprehend the content of the sentence he attempts to analyze. It often happens, however, that pupils will correctly diagram and parse a sentence the meaning of which is wholly unintelligible to them. It is even possible to parse and diagram a thing in the form of a sentence, which has no meaning, as : "The correlated violet, tenderly squaring its family circle which had long bristled with grim-visaged dactyls, respectfully blended into the empyrean." But we need not go to the realm of nonsense for material which children may parse and diagram by rote :

> " Carelessly I roamed
> As through a wide museum, from whose stores
> A casual rarity is singled out
> And has its brief perusal."—*Wordsworth.*

This, I am confident, may be disposed of according to the strict tenets of the book, by pupils to whom "carelessly," as here used, "museum," "stores," "casual," "rarity," "singled," and "perusal," mean next to nothing. They can parse these words, can name the class of the sentence, select subjects, predicates, modifiers, and can arrange the whole into a diagram.

I am not even hinting that the daily work in parsing and analysis is largely of this kind, but there is some of it, and we cannot afford the waste. By the time pupils have passed through the eighth year of school, and have given two or three years to grammar, they have, as a rule, laid up in memory the usual technicalities, and have learned to look for the thought relations in a sentence as guides to its analysis and parsing ; but for this skill in dissection they have paid a great price, and it is far from general to find it supplemented by skill in combination. Not construction but destruction is too commonly the " destined end and way." [1]

What of their ability to read distinctly and persuasively, so that the listener hears, comprehends, feels; is informed, pleased, moved to action?

As this implies an alert eye, a quick mental grip, a normal set of vocal organs under control, a ready knowledge of the words used, the power to hide the effort of taking in the word and its meaning, a constant appreciation of what is due to one's hearers, it is exactly the reverse of an easy task. I am not speaking of mere parrot imitations, but of real reading; and I am forced to the conclusion that the result is far below what it should be, considering the eight years of ostensible practice. There are schools and schools, but the pupil who reads well, so as to satisfy, not the fond parent who is likely to be charmed without discrimination over the performance of his child, but the semi-critical stranger who wishes to apprehend what is read, is likely to be a member of a household where books are the choicest furniture, and reading a daily and nightly mode of employment and enjoyment. I do not forget that in many instances the reading aloud, by the child, of the book he has carried home is the only spiritual entertainment afforded in that household.

If we wish to sound our pupils, to note their attainment as readers, we need not limit our investigations

---

[1] Is it not true that the good that children are expected to get, and sometimes do get, from the study of grammar, can be obtained more readily and rationally through reading and writing?

to the class about to go into the high school.   Try those pupils whose essays and orations have not been drilled upon, and the depressing conclusion must be reached that into the happy kingdom of approved good readers many are called, but few accept the invitation.

In the first years of school life much of what passes for reading is mere reciting from memory, in which there is not even recognition of words, to say nothing of catching the writer's thought, and the evidence is irresistible that all along the way there is much repetition of words without knowledge.

Reading demands unceasing use of eye, memory, judgment, and imagination ; while children of all ages yield so unresistingly to the sin of carelessness, that in cases beyond number the reader finds things which the writer did not say, and fails to find things that he did say.

Recently I saw upon a blackboard a problem of this form : Multiply the sum of a and b by c, and subtract the product from d.   The teacher said that the pupils had by no means all solved it.   When questioned they showed a knowledge of the import of " sum," " product," " difference," and they could add, multiply, and subtract.   They had failed to perform the operations from a lack of the power of continuous attention needed to read the sentence properly.   What teacher and what examiner has escaped similar experiences ? Perhaps training in reading problems, without thought of present solution, simply to *learn* to read them, would be a fruitful exercise.

Is the fact that one has memorized a paragraph in geography or in history or in physiology convincing

proof that he has read it, has caught its message ?
Many there be who harbor a suspicion that the passage
means something, but have no yearning to find it
out. In happy-go-lucky mood they seize upon the
first notion that rises to the surface. The knowl-
edge acquired is likely to be a mixture of fact and
absurdity.

The following are genuine examples. The class had
read—studied—their lesson in geography, and had
made notes of what they thought they had found
therein. In the text the terms " penal colony,"
" cereals," and " native gold " were used.

" A penal colony is one that was formed after the
thirteen colonies ; is a colony where punishment is
denounced ; is a colony wherein all the transgressors
of the law are exiled to some other country ; is a
machine in which the colony put people when they
disobey the law ; is a small colony ; is under a coun-
try which punishes the colony when she wants to."

" Cereals are formed by the salt water of the sea ;
are the principal products of a country ; are such crops
as lettuce, celery, etc. ; are things dug from the
earth."

" Native gold is gold found in small quantities in
mountains and rivers where no one knows where
it is ; is gold raised in a native country ; is gold
produced by the country in which you live ; is gold
that was discovered by the natives; is gold that
always was there."

An " interpretation " of the statement that " much
of the soil of Ohio is of foreign origin " was " so
many foreigners come to Ohio with dirty shoes."

This "disease of not listening," this " malady of

not marking" the writer's exact meaning, seems to be very general, but we may hope it is not incurable.

It is a very bad mental habit for one to read simply for the sake of reading, to feel whatever of pleasure there may be in the sensation caused by the words passing before the eye, and, it may be, off the tongue. Perhaps it is wrong to call it a " mental " habit ; and without doubt it does great harm in that it hangs a screen about the thought of the writer. Persisted in, the practice will make real reading an impossible art.   When we look it squarely in the face, the com- mon reading recitation appears a sad business ; for every sentence that a pupil reads, indifferent to its meaning or with his mind's eye half-closed to the fact that it has meaning, does its share of mischief.

It is a matter of general observation that the speech of pupils, and also of their elders, when it follows grammatical rules, does not consciously do so because of personal study of those rules ; that it is, whether correct or incorrect, mainly the result of conscious and unconscious imitation.   When one listens to the work- ing models of street and playground ; of the home of the average boy ; of—sad to hint it—a more than occa- sional schoolroom with its "have saw," "had ought," "you was," "leave it lay," "between you and I," "they want you and I," he can infer the free-hand English of a lamentable per cent. of young Amer- icans.

And those whose duty it is to read somewhat search- ingly the written work of pupils, if they are sensi- tive to the difference between a tolerable paragraph and an excellent one, will bear out my assertion that the skill of pupils in this art of written expression is far less than that which they bring to the processes of analysis and parsing.

It seems not a rash or unkind conclusion that there is urgent need that our schools should better their instruction in English ; and with an eye upon the grades below the high school I wish to consider the question how this may be done.

IN order that instruction in English in the elementary schools may be greatly improved, there is one comprehensive need. The subject in its twofold phase of (1) reading—silent and oral,—and (2) expression—oral and written—must attain a very much higher place in the estimation of those who formulate courses of study and those who oversee the carrying out of courses of study ; of those who license teachers, those who employ teachers, and those who instruct teachers in their institutes ; of, finally and vitally, teachers themselves.

I have seen several courses of study which would not rouse a suspicion that reading and writing are paramount in importance ; that grammar and spelling and other language studies are simply aids to the attainment of a mastery of these two. In these courses of study the ability to teach reading and composition is taken for granted. When English as a branch of instruction in school shall have come to its own, it will have a much larger share of the day, and will also have its precious minutes more wisely spent.

Suppose it is oral reading in the fifth, sixth or seventh school year we have in mind, did you ever apply a little "number work" to find about how much time in the round year a pupil spends in drill? My figuring gives something less than six hours. In the eight years which lead him to the high school he,

Read. and Comp.—2. 17

possibly, reads to the presumedly critical ear of his teacher about one and a half days.   Is it strange, then, that he should fail to learn an art so difficult as this ?

Very much more time should be given by the teacher to prepare himself for conducting the reading exercise and the writing or composition exercise—this refers to the special preparation—and what a wide field of literature, of history, of elementary science and nature study, of elocution in the proper sense of that term, must be carefully cultivated by one who aspires to the high position of teacher of a reading class !

In the reading books which children use at school there are many lessons that speak from the heart of nature, and only the teacher who is in sympathy with nature, who possesses a love that begets knowledge, can do a teacher's part by his flock when he leads them into these green pastures.   He need not be a scientist, but he must have acquaintance with hundreds of the inhabitants, animal and vegetable, of the earth, the air, the water :

> " Hast thou named all the birds without a gun ?
> Loved the wood rose and left it on its stalk ?
>
> .   .   .
>
> Oh, be my friend, and teach me to be thine ! "

Among the things that are indispensable to a radical change for the better in the reading and writing of our schools, the following may be mentioned :

1. Higher estimation of the prime importance of these arts.

2. Better economy of time, devoting less of it to the subordinate branches and more to the higher ; a realization that spelling and language lessons and grammar

have their chief function in enabling the student to read and to write.

3. More thorough preparation on the part of teachers.

4. Smaller classes, so that each pupil may be led or driven to do some of his very best work every day of his school life ; part of his work should be at least the effort to express in good form a few related thoughts of his own upon a given subject.

Let us pass before our minds some of the exercises which we call oral reading :

1. When a person with his eye upon the page pronounces the words in their order and with a fair degree of correctness, occasionally checking his rate of motion to indicate that he has sighted a period, he is said to read.

2. The next person does what the former did, and also by dint of emphasis gives unity to each phrase or clause, as by proper accent he gives unity to a long word. The hearer, in this case, has a much easier task to grasp the thought in the writer's mind or to know what emotion moves him. He is pitiful, or impatient, or grateful, or angry. His words suggest it.

3. The reader who now takes the book steps easily in the path well-worn by his predecessors. He pronounces the words as good usage dictates, and uses emphasis as the sense directs him ; but he does more. He enters into the mind of the writer and turns his written sentences into speech. The thought and the emotion determine the pitch of the voice, the rate of movement, the force of utterance, the quality of tone, the glidings or inflections which, with no change

of word, may turn consent to refusal, approval to con-
demnation, doubt to confidence, white to black. The
hearer's task is now so slight that he is unconscious
of it. He sees the thought, not darkly as it might
have appeared had he even read the language him-
self, but face to face through the reader's transparent
interpretation. He is now not simply aware that the
writer is happy over some glad occasion ; he himself
is glad. It is not now an inference that the writer is
in trouble ; a tear of sympathy is in the hearer's
eye.

That summit we may not expect to attain, but
this is the direction for our striving ; and many
teachers mount to cheering prospects, not by sudden
flight, but by toil while their companions sleep.

IT is far from my purpose to urge that text-book rhetoric be taught in elementary schools, but I believe that some of the marrow of it can be extracted by the reading class. Its comprehensive theme is style, and style is the way writers say things.

I do not recall the fact that any teacher of mine ever intimated to his pupils that one sentence in a book was not as well written as another, that our incorrect analysis and feeble expression might possibly be the author's fault, and that if a certain paragraph were made clearer, more forcible, more musical, it would be more easily read and would need no diagram.

No doubt it is better in the main to study pieces of the best quality, but an occasional criticism, using this word in its common but incorrect sense, will arouse interest in the class and cause them to place a higher estimate upon good English by contrast.

Suppose a teacher of pupils in the seventh or eighth grade finds in the reading which his pupils are to do,— that is, in the English from the study of which they are to gain some benefit,—a passage like this :

"A pretty little fawn had been brought in from the woods when very young, and nursed and petted by a lady in the village until it had become as tame as possible. . . . One morning, after playing about as usual until weary, it lay down in the sunshine, at the feet of one of its friends, upon the steps of a store. There

21

came along a countryman, who for several years had
been a hunter by pursuit, and who still kept several
hounds, one of which was now with him."

I should hope, as teacher, to lead my class to see
that the expression "as possible" weakens the first
sentence, and it would perhaps be better thus, "had
become quite tame;" that the word "about" in
"playing about as usual," looks in both directions;
that the countryman had been a hunter "for several
years" is nothing to the story, and that "hunter by
pursuit" sounds like a perverted pun.

"   In another instant, before the spectators had
thought of the danger, and before its friends could se-
cure it, the fawn was bounding away through the
street, and the hound in full chase. The bystanders
were eager to save it; several persons immediately
followed its track; the friends who had long fed and
fondled it, calling the name it had hitherto known, in
vain."

Are "spectators," "friends," "bystanders," "per-
sons," four groups, or three, or two ? (Several persons
followed its track over a course which it ran in less
than *half-a-minute*, and when it dashed onwards
towards the lake, it threw itself into the water,
through which the hound followed it *by the scent*.)

Would it be pardonable to rewrite the sentence
quoted ?—"Before the friends of the fawn realized
its danger, it bounded away, with the hound in full
chase, but, eager to save it, they followed at their best
speed, vainly calling its name."

As an exercise akin to this—it is composition also,
the material being furnished—the teacher may change
the faultless arrangement of words or phrases which

make up a sentence, and submit his revision to the class for criticism. He presents them this ·—" By the side of a blackberry bush there was a bush sparrow's nest daintily bowered in the grass on a green slope, and two yellow-breasted chats had placed their grassy cradle hard by, and by their loud cries of warning to keep away proclaimed to all the world their secret." Grammatical I believe ; rhythm not good ; the echo of "bush" and "bush," and of "by" and "by," not pleasant to the ear.

Before he remodeled it for the worse the sentence had this form : " On a green slope was a bush sparrow's nest, daintily bowered in the grass by the side of a blackberry bush, and in a thicket hard by two yellow-breasted chats had placed their cradle, proclaiming their secret to all the world by their loud cries of warning to keep away." Note how much more smoothly it reads, yet, does not " proclaiming " suggest at first that it was the placing that proclaimed ? This error must be corrected when the reader comes to the real mode of proclamation, " their loud cries." Does the following improve it ? . . . " had placed their grassy cradle, but by their loud cries of warning to keep away, they proclaimed their secret to all the world." The reason for introducing " but " is the contrast between the hiding of the nest and their loud cries which advertise it. Between "warning" and " to keep away " the reader's eye flashes out toward a possible intruder.

Are these things not to some extent matters of individual taste ? Verily. But I am trying to teach the gospel of careful reading, of a cultivation of a taste for good English, of persistent effort to train boys and girls to write it, and I believe that such exercises as I am sketching will do something toward the attainment of these ends.

I have said that style is the way writers say things. We are told also that "the style is the man." No two persons state an argument, describe a wooded hillside, give utterance to an emotion, in exactly the same way. There is something in each writer's "way" that cannot be taught. While these things are true, it is also true that certain very important lessons can be learned by closely attending to the structure of writings that have the world's stamp of approval upon them, and of these lessons use can be made. (1) The first element of a good style is clearness. The words may be too few and hence fail to express the meaning, while too many tend to obscure it. (2) The second element is forcefulness. The vital words, those which call for emphasis, must not be allowed to lurk in holes and corners where they will partly escape notice. (3) The third element is a judicious choice of words with due care for their good repute and their fitness to express the thought. (4) The fourth element consists of a distribution of the accented syllables such that the voice may do its part with grace and ease. It is concerned over a judicious mingling of long and short words, of strong and weak syllables. In other words, it is rhythmic, and not only yields itself to the molding power of the vocal organs, but the soul in some strange way hears the music through the voice of the reader. In obedience to this principle the echoing of sounds not called for in rhyming should be avoided.

IV. RHYTHM.

IN teaching children to read, the matter of rhythm must not be neglected, though it sometimes has scant attention even on the part of writers, and their neglect leaves the resulting sentence or paragraph harder to read effectively. It is not my purpose to discuss what rhythm in prose is, but I shall aim to aid the teacher who wishes to be somewhat surer of his footing upon the poems which the children are to read. They may well be spared the most of the names and all the definitions of formal prosody, which the observing boy defined as "that part of the grammar that's always so clean," but their teacher should have the meter of the poem singing in his ear. It is an essential part of the lesson. It is not a difficult thing to learn. It requires, in most cases, only a following of the direction often seen at railway crossings: "Stop, look, and listen."

Let every pupil of the class listen for the accents while some one reads aloud a stanza, and let there be a count of syllables to the foot and of feet to the line. It would be putting to good use a corner of the blackboard to write upon it the names and the markings of these poetic measures as we find them :

IAMBUS · TROCHEE ‾ ˇ ; DACTYL ‾ · SPONDEE – ;
ANAPEST . ; AMPHIBRACH ˇ ‾ ˇ [1]

[1] An accented, or long syllable, is represented by ‾; an unaccented, or short syllable, by ˇ. The cesural pause is represented by |.

25

We shall find that verse writers very often use two kinds of feet in the same stanza, and not seldom in the same line. Suppose we examine a number of lines found in certain familiar poems, and mark them:

1. Thĕ spīd | ĕr wears | ă plāīn | brŏwn drēss |
2. Clōūds thăt | wāndĕr | thrōūgh thĕ | skȳ |
3. Soon ăs thĕ | leaves hĕard thĕ | wīnds lŏud căll |
4. Făr dōwn | ĭn thĕ văl | lĕy thĕ whēāt | grŏws dēēp |

1. Shĕ hād | ă rūs | tĭc, wōōd | lănd aīr |
2. Thĕ nīght | wăs dārk | thĕ sūn | wăs hīd |
3. Thīs ĭs | thĕ wāy | thĕ mōrn | ĭng dāwns |
4. Ĭ wĭll tēll | yŏu thĕ stō | rȳ ŏf thrēē | lĭttlĕ mīce
   Ĭf yōu | wĭll kĕĕp stĭll | ănd līs | tĕn tŏ mē |
5. Frŏm her bright | eăr pārt | ĕd thĕ cūrls | ŏf gōld |
6. Fāthĕr | Tīme, yŏur | fōōtstĕps | gō |

1. Jŭst ăcrōss | thĕ rōad | bȳ thĕ chēr | rȳ trees |
2. One lĭttlĕ | sāndpĭpĕr | ănd Ī |
3. Cōmrăde | whēre wĭlt | thŏu bē | tŏ-nīght ? |
4. Bŭt whāt | măkes thēē seem | sŏ ŭncōn | scīous ŏf cāre ? |
5. Bŭt ōh | fŏr thĕ tōuch | ŏf ă vān | ĭshed hānd |
6. Thĕre's ă māg | ĭcăl īsle | ŭp thĕ rīv | ĕr ŏf Tīme |
7. Mērrĭlȳ | swīngĭng ŏn | brīĕr ănd | wēēd |
8. Mēānwhĭle hăd | sprēad ĭn thĕ | vīllăge | thĕ | tīdĭngs ŏf | ĭll, ănd ŏn | āll sīdes |
   Wāndērĕd, | wāilĭng, frŏm | hōuse tō | hōuse | thē | wōmĕn ănd | chĭldrĕn. |
   Lōng ăt hĕr | fāthĕr's | dōōr ‖ Ē | vāngĕlinĕ | stōōd wĭth hĕr | rīght hānd |

Shīeldĭng hĕr | ēyes frŏm thĕ | lĕvēl | rāys ŏf thĕ |
  . sūn, ‖ thăt, dŏ | scēndĭng |
Lĭghtĕd thĕ | vīllāge | strēēt ‖ wĭth mўs | tērĭoŭs |
  splēndŏr, ănd | rōōfed ēach |
Pḙaṣānt's | cōttăge wĭth | gōldēn | thātch, | ănd ĕm |
  blāzŏned ĭts | wīndōws |

The meter of "Evangeline," the favorite and beau-
tiful poem from which these lines are taken, requires
close attention on the part of teacher and class, if they
would get the true melody, if they would see some-
thing of what Longfellow aimed to do in the structure
of the poem.

They will observe that each line is composed of six
feet,—dactyls and spondees. In the latter, each of the
two syllables should have full time. Each line ends
with a spondee, as "all sides," "children," "right
hand." The foot before the last must be a dactyl, the
other four may be the one or the other. What is
known as the *cesura* is much oftener found in the
third foot than elsewhere, though in this quotation
it is once in the fourth and once in the fifth. The
cesura is a "sense pause." It is at the end of a word
and in the midst of a foot. In this quotation it comes
after "village," "house" (the second), "door," "sun,"
"street," and "thatch."

Frequently the proper mode of accenting a word is
learned by correctly reading a verse in which it occurs
and noting the way in which the poet uses it. Some
examples of this are here given :

1. Fair is proud Se'ville ; let her country boast—
2. Let us alone to guard Cori'oli.

3. From off the rock Tarpe'ian, never more—
4. Go, Pin'darus, get higher on that hill—
5. Ride, ride, Messa'la, ride, and give these bills—
6. They mean to warn us at Philip'pi here—
7. If ever you should come to Mo'dena—
8. Where Fornari'na's fair young face—
9. With it Camo'ens soothed an exile's grief—
10. O'er the precipice plunging downward
    Gleamed like Ish'koodah, the comet.
11. And chas'tisement doth therefore hide his head.
12. As fair Alcy'one with anguish pressed.

Pleasant things are said of the uses of variety, its relation to interest, attention, apprehension, memory.

The older pupils might be encouraged to look into good prose and find a sequence of syllables, a sentence it may be, wherein the rhythm would be identical with some one of the lines quoted above. The hunt need not take them far or long.

1. Thĕ ēvenĭng | ŏf thĕ fīfth | cāme ōn |
   —*Bancroft.*
2. The young moon | was shin | ing brightly |
   In a cloud | less win | ter sky ; |
And its light | was increased | by a new- | fallen snow |
   —*Bancroft.*
3. Parties of | soldiers were | driving | about |
   —*Bancroft.*
4. There are streaks | of light | in a thun | der cloud |
   —*Landor.*
5. Nature de | scends down to | infinite | smallness |
   —*S. Smith.*
6. Nothing could | stop that as | tonishing | infantry |
   —*Napier.*

For the novelty of the thing and the flavor which can be got from it, an exercise in rhythm might be given, once in a long while, after this fashion : Select a bit of good strong prose, and let the game be to turn it with the slightest change of words into the form of blank verse. Mark, I do not say into poetry.

Here is a sentence of Thoreau's. The reader of his essay upon Nature's way of planting trees will recognize it :

> Whēn yŏu | cŭt dōwn | ăn oăk | ă pīne | wĭll nōt |
> At once | spring up, | unless | there are | or were |
> Quite re | cently, | seed-bear | ing pines | near by |
> Which send | their seeds | upon | the wind | to where |
> The oak | had stood. |

Is this poetry ? The eye reports that the lines begin with capitals ; the ear, that each, after the first, contains five iambic feet ; the taste, that every word in it is fit for use in poetry. The cutting down of the oak ; the pine, launching its seed upon the wind, are pastoral incidents which suggest a pleasing environment. What is lacking ?

Following is a part of " A Pen Picture " by William Black :

> By Lavender had Sheila been transformed
> To a heroine in the half hour of their stroll ;
> And as they sat at dinner on this eve
> He clothed her in the garments of romance.
> Her father with heavy brow and great gray beard
> Became the King of Thule, living in
> This solitary house looking o'er the sea.
> His daughter, the Princess, had the glamor
> Of a thousand legends dwelling in her eyes ;

And when she walked by the Atlantic shore,
Now growing yellow under the western sun,
In the wonder of her face strange thoughts appeared.

For another device worth a lesson or two in teaching correct notions in movement, or rhythm, select a portion of blank verse, or a rhyming stanza, write it as prose, making only the needed verbal changes, and disguising the rhyme, then submit your prose to the pupils for restoration to its original form.

Here is an example or two of each kind :

1. I look forth over the boundless blue, where joyously the bright crests of innumerable waves glance to the sun at once, as when the hands of a great multitude are upward flung in acclamation.—*Bryant.*

(Remember that there are such things as broken lines ; the first three words are one.)

2. Under my eye, in its flowing the blue river chimes clearly ; and the south winds, warmly and broadly, over the sky are blowing.—*Tennyson.*

(Two pairs of rhymes.   Start with " Clearly.")

3. Within the old farm-house we sat.   Its windows overlooking the bay, gave, day and night, an easy entrance to the damp cold sea-breeze.—*Longfellow.*

(Two pairs of rhymes.)

4. Here the idle shepherd leans on his crook and vacantly does look on the rippling waves, that peaceful still flow 'twixt bitterest foemen.—*Byron.*

(Three lines, first two rhyme.)

5. From the shore there breathes a living fragrance of flowers yet fresh with childhood ; the light drip of the suspended oar drops on the ear, or the grasshopper chirps one more good-night carol.—*Byron.*

(Four lines, three of them rhyme.)

6. It (the Marsh) lies, a dim world, by itself, between the sea and the wood. The feet of pilgrim streams travel silently across it ; also vagrant mists which smirch the purple cloak of evening like a drifting smoke. (Six lines, two rhymes.)

When summer noon is gold on fern and brake, and when red brands from the fires of sunset burn within its black pools, it is a strange, still place. (Four lines, one rhyme.)

Within its mossy glooms white violets, like lost pearls, lie hid, and tall rushes sway their soft silken plumes on the wandering breeze.—*Susan Hartley Coolidge.*

(Four lines, one rhyme.)

In the following quotations from Blackmore's "Lorna Doone," there have been no verbal changes as there were in the selections from Thoreau and Black. The matter is here simply given in the guise of poetry rather than of prose :

1. All the earth was flat with snow,
   All the air was thick with snow ;
   More than this no man could see,
   For all the world was snowing.

2. Ever and again the tempest snatched
   Little whiffs from the channeled edge,
   Twirled them round and made them dance,
   Over the chine of the monster pile,
   Then let them lie like herring-bones,
   Or the seams of sand where the tide has been.

3. Not a sign of life was moving,
   Nor was any change of view,
   Unless the wild wind struck the crest,
   Of some cold drift and bowed it.

4. Then I thought of promise fair,
   Such as glowed around me

Where the red rocks held the sun
When he was departed.
But as evening spread across them,
Shading with a silent fold,
All the color stole away,
All remembrance waned and died.

THE teacher who wishes to use the reading matter of the grades as literature, must not only drill his class in oral expression, but must lead them to detect the writer's thought and feeling, and to see that this has much to do with both the composition and the oral reading. He must train them also to recognize the story or the nature paragraph as true, because it harmonizes with something they have felt or seen.

The phrase, a knowledge of literature, conjures up a series of concentric circles. Within the one of shortest radius is the literature that a reader actually has made his own. He carries it about with him, or, better, it has come to be a part of him. Like a wiser self it speaks to him, a word of warning betimes, a voice of gladness for his gayer hours, and of healing for his darker musings.

The next circumference includes not only those wise and beautiful things which have established themselves verbally in memory, but all the books thoughtfully read, into which "a man has gone in the making."

At a great distance is the last circle, and within its extended limits is all that the reader remembers about authors, their styles, characteristics, the books they wrote and how they came to write them, their close companions, their social environment, the great

Read. and Comp.—3. **33**

affairs of the world which gave special stimulus to their thought and its expression.

Here I shall try to put into shape the apparent reasons for urging upon the reader, whether pupil or teacher, to form a habit of memorizing lines, stanzas, poems, paragraphs, which breathe the breath of life,— of gathering into memory's

> "pictured urn
> Thoughts that breathe, and words that burn."

Much has been written about books as companions; but, in active life, if your author is to help you directly, you must know exactly what he said, not merely remember vaguely that in a certain book he said something which would suit your present purpose. James Russell Lowell once made a graphic illustration of the advantage the shillalah has over certain other weapons in being always loaded.

Another valuable result of this practice is the enriching of the reader's vocabulary, for these fine words are not too good for human nature's daily use. The validity of this reason is proved when boys and girls use correctly single words which had found entrance to their mental store in a memory lesson.

I would not lay great stress upon this practice as a means of cultivating the memory, for I am not convinced that it makes a man more sure of his facts and his dates in history; of the names of people, if he be a politician or a salesman; of his list of commissions down town, if he be the head of a household. But it gives practice in the art of paying minute attention; it exercises judgment upon the question, why has not some unbidden verbal guest a right to stay? it quickens taste into an ardor which will seize upon the beautiful, the elegant, the excellent in this realm of art, and will aid it to apprehend these qualities in other realms.

The process of closely attending to, of cherishing in the heart, of repeatedly recalling the language which enshrines the good, the true, the beautiful, will have an uplifting influence, a refining tendency upon character, which grows by what it feeds on. The song that is to thrill and inspire must be cherished in the memory, not merely be found in the book upon one's shelf.

Upon this emotional culture I lay emphasis as the choicest fruit of this habit; and I would make it a habit, not a matter of occasion. It may well begin in the first year at school ; there is no good reason why it should ever end.   Teachers who have not tried it may begrudge the expenditure of time ; but begun early, followed persistently, it will surprise one to note the small demands the practice makes upon time and labor. The presentation upon the blackboard of a new stanza from a new poem for this kind of study may be like the unrolling of a beautiful picture to delight the eyes of the children.   Whether it will be such depends, like the success of every other effort of the schoolroom, upon that fundamental condition, the teacher.   I remember well the joy that shone from fifty primary faces in one schoolroom while the teacher read and illustrated Helen Hunt Jackson's "September."   The children knew nothing about the stated laws of optics, but they saw both the "asters by the brook-side" and the "asters in the brook."   Later in the season, the study of the "Fringed Gentian" aroused such interest that the boys in several classes made a successful search for the rare flower which is the theme of Bryant's pretty and devout little poem, and their zeal had to be moderated to protect the flower.

For this use I would prefer the literature of nature to begin with, while the birds sing and the flowers bloom, or the wind roars and the snow falls. In the case above mentioned, one who has not seen the gentian can hardly enjoy the full meaning of the poem, and one who is ignorant of the poem will miss something of the gentian's lesson of beauty ; for "Beauty is truth, truth beauty," and entering into Keats's conception of beauty, I would say that that is the supreme characteristic of literature which is to be absorbed, assimilated, memorized.

Soon other threads than nature should be woven into this spiritual web ; writings should be used whose spirit is love of home, friends, country, humanity, God. Religion, patriotism, piety, reign more royally in the heart from having found worthy expression ; and the writers, like so many Prosperos,

> " Took pains to make thee speak, taught thee each hour
> One thing or other ; when thou did'st not, savage,
> Know thine own meaning,   I endow'd thy purposes
> With words that made them known."

I append here a list of selections which are worthy to be memorized. From actual experience this memory exercise has been found to demand but a few minutes daily for its accomplishment, with an occasional question as to meaning. The selections should not be rigidly molded into a book of elegant extracts, but varied as taste and circumstance may dictate.

POEMS FOR MEMORIZING.

Year I.

1. September.—*Helen Hunt Jackson.*
2. Lullaby.—*Tennyson.*
3. The Rainbow.—*Wordsworth.*
4. The Mountain and the Squirrel.—*Emerson.*
5. Shadow-town Ferry.—*Anonymous.*

Year II.

1. Reviews.
2. What the Winds Bring.—*Steadman.*
3. The Wind and the Leaves.—*Cowper.*
4. The Moon.—*Mrs. Follen.*
5. America.—*S. F. Smith.*

Year III.

1. Reviews.
2. The Fiftieth Birthday of Agassiz.—*Longfellow.*
3. Aladdin.—*Lowell.*
4. The Nightingale and Glowworm.—*Cowper.*
5. October's Bright Blue Weather.—*Helen Hunt Jackson.*
6. April Weather.—*Celia Thaxter.*

Year IV.

1. Reviews.
2. The Brown Thrush.—*Lucy Larcom.*
3. The Rain (in part).—*Longfellow.*
4. The Gladness of Nature.—*Bryant.*
5. In Time's Swing.—*Lucy Larcom.*
6. The Sandpiper.—*Celia Thaxter.*
7. There is a Land.—*Montgomery.*

Year V.

1. Reviews.
2. Daffodils.—*Wordsworth.*
3. To the Fringed Gentian.—*Bryant.*
4. The Skylark.—*Hogg.*
5. The Old Oaken Bucket.—*Woodworth.*
6. Freaks of the Frost.—*Miss Gould.*
7. The Village Blacksmith.—*Longfellow.*

Year VI.

1. Reviews.
2. Abou Ben Adhem.—*Leigh Hunt.*
3. Death of the Flowers.—*Bryant.*
4. Field Preaching.—*Phœbe Cary.*
5. The Beggar.—*Lowell.*
6. Paul Revere's Ride.—*Longfellow.*
7. The Last Leaf.—*Holmes.*
8. The Landing of the Pilgrims.—*Mrs. Hemans.*

Year VII.

1. Reviews.
2. To a Waterfowl.—*Bryant.*
3. The Cloud.—*Shelley.*
4. Each and All.—*Emerson.*
5. The Battle of Waterloo.—*Byron.*
6. The Rhodora.—*Emerson.*
7. The Mountain Daisy.—*Burns.*
8. The Song of the Potter.—*Longfellow*

Year VIII.

1. Reviews.
2. *a.* "The quality of mercy is not strained." (14 lines)—"The Merchant of Venice", Act IV., Scene 1.

     b. "So shaken as we are, so wan with care" (18 lines).—"Henry IV.", Part I., Act I., Scene 1.

     c. "Farewell, a long farewell, to all my greatness!" (22 lines). "Henry VIII.", Act III., Scene 2.

     d. "Friends, Romans, Countrymen" (35 lines).—"Julius Cæsar", Act III., Scene II.

     e. "Speak the speech, I pray you" (entire).—"Hamlet", Act III., Scene 2.

     f. "Our revels now are ended" (11 lines).—"The Tempest", Act IV., Scene 1.

     g. "Most potent, grave, and reverend signors" (19 lines).—"Othello", Act I., Scene 3.

3. Thanatopsis.—*Bryant.*
4. The Chambered Nautilus.—*Holmes.*
5. Break, Break, Break.—*Tennyson.*

MEMORIZING PROSE.

It is true that the highest literature of a language is embodied in its poetry, and also true that to memorize poetry is much easier than to memorize prose, yet our choice of literature for this intimate study should not be restricted to poems. There are mental treasures to be found in prose, and he who finds and makes them his own is doing something toward the attainment of a knowledge of what fine prose is, toward the growth of a pure taste in language; he is securing a touchstone with which to test what he reads. Such passages and sentences, may be found occasionally in the reading lessons, but not on every page; indeed, we may go sometimes a long way without finding one. In the teacher's general reading he will come upon coins of this perfect mintage, which may be brought to the class with whatever of the context is needed to show their significance. The following are some of these :

1. " The season was far advanced. On the bare limbs of the forest hung a few withered remnants of its gay autumnal livery ; and the smoke crept upward through the sullen November air from the squalid wigwams of La Salle's allies."—*Francis Parkman.*

2. " It is only by the contrast of some slight noise that we can appreciate silence. A solitude is never so lonely as when the wind sighs through it."—*Lowell.*

3. " With a tale the poet cometh unto you,—with a tale which holdeth children from play, and old men from the chimney-corner."—*Sir Philip Sidney.*"

4. " As long as he lived he was the guiding-star of a whole brave nation, and when he died the little children cried in the streets."—*Motley*, (speaking of William the Silent).

5. " Standing alone in that fair solitude, as much alone as on some atoll in a distant sea, I felt as though I might know man better, see him in clearer lights, if I could live apart from him longer in such still, calm, holy places as Indian Brook canyon." —*Frank Bolles.*

6. " Every winter the liquid and trembling surface of Walden pond, which was so sensitive to every breath, and reflected every light and shadow, becomes solid to the depth of a foot or a foot and a half, so that it will support the heaviest teams, and perchance snow covers it to an equal depth, and it is not to be distinguished from any level field. I cut my way first through a foot of snow, and then a foot of ice, and open a window under my feet, where, kneeling to drink, I look down into the quiet parlor of the fishes with its softened light and its bright sanded floor ; there a perennial waveless serenity reigns as in the amber twilight sky, corresponding to the cool and even temperament of the inhabitants. Heaven is under our feet as well as over our heads."—*Thoreau.*

7. " When the casement rattles in the gust, and the snow-

flakes pelt hard against the window panes, then I spread out my sheet of paper, with the certainty that thoughts and fancies will gleam forth upon it like stars at twilight, or like violets in May,—perhaps to fade as soon.

Turn we again to the fireside, and sit musing there, lending our ears to the wind, till perhaps it shall seem like an articulate voice, and dictate wild and airy matter for the pen."
—*Hawthorne.*

8. " Winter had set in along the St. Lawrence, and already dead Nature was sheeted in funereal white. Lakes and ponds were frozen, rivulets sealed up, the black rocks and the black trunks of the pine trees were beplastered with snow, and its heavy masses crushed the dull green boughs into the drifts beneath. The forest was silent as the grave."—*Francis Parkman.*

" Apples, these I mean, unspeakably fair ; some freckled all over on the stem side with fine crimson spots on a white ground, as if accidentally sprinkled from the brush of Him who paints the autumn leaves. Others, again, are sometimes red inside, perfused with a beautiful blush, fairy food, too beautiful to eat,—apple of the evening sky ! But like shells and pebbles on the seashore, they must be seen as they sparkle amid the withering leaves in some dell in the woods, in the autumnal air, or as they lie in the wet grass."—*Thoreau.*

" Multitudes of bees used to bury themselves in the yellow blossoms of the summer squashes. This, too, was a deep satisfaction ; although when they had laden themselves with sweets they flew away to some unknown hive, which would give back nothing in requital of what my garden had contributed. But I was glad thus to fling a benefaction upon the passing breeze, with the certainty that somebody must profit by it, and that there would be a little more honey in the world to allay the sourness and bitterness which mankind is always complaining of. Yes, indeed ; my life was the sweeter for that honey."—*Hawthorne.*

9. " Blessed was the sunshine when it came again at the close of another stormy day, beaming from the edge of the western

horizon ; while the massive firmament of clouds threw down all the gloom it could, but served only to kindle the golden light into a more brilliant glow by the strongly-contrasted shadows."—*Hawthorne*.

10. " To the body and mind which have been cramped by noxious work or company, nature is medicinal and restores their tone. The tradesman, the attorney, comes out of the din and craft of the street and sees the sky and the woods, and is a man again. In their eternal calm he finds himself. The health of the eye seems to demand a horizon. We are never tired, so long as we can see far enough. . . .

" I see the spectacle of morning from the hill-top over against my house, from daybreak to sunrise, with emotions which an angel might share. The long, slender bars of cloud float like fishes in the sea of crimson light. From the earth, as a shore, I looked out into that silent sea. I seem to partake its rapid transformations ; the active enchantment reaches my dust, and I dilate and conspire with the morning wind. Give me health and a day, and I will make the pomp of emperors ridiculous."—*Emerson*.

VI. COMPOSITION.

UPON this subject there are many excellent text-books, and I have no intention of entering upon a general discussion of the subject. My leading thought has been already expressed ; namely, the urgent need for teachers to stop and take a steady look at the prime necessity of the thing. These boys and girls whom we are trying to educate will need during their entire life the ability to utter with their tongues and to write upon paper the words which body forth the thoughts that arise in them ; and all the "laborious days" spent in their instruction have but an impotent conclusion unless our pupils shall acquire this ability to express themselves clearly and correctly upon any subject of which they have knowledge, or upon which they are capable of doing some consecutive thinking.

The oral recitation should count for much more than it does as an intelligent conversation exercise. Conversations upon given subjects should be frequent, should be conscientiously prepared for, and earnestly conducted. Current events of interest and worthy of careful reading about may profitably be made topics for oral compositions. These might be seconded by written essays upon the same topics. Unless pupils have abundant practise in framing sentences to express something which they have to say, they will not be likely to attain the art of writing or speaking good English. Rules and models can not yield this result.

In the early stages of practice in the art of making good sentences an artifice like the following may be tried. It will show the young writers some of the signs which indicate where a sentence may or must end, and will teach them much of practical syntax.

The teacher writes upon the blackboard a number of words in proper sequence, and challenges the class to continue it in as many ways as their various tastes and inventive powers may prompt, and their acquaintance with their native tongue may allow. As an example, the blackboard shows :

Little Bell took up her basket

There is no period at the end ; the sentence is to continue ; and when you have made Harry and Nellie, for instance, understand that the next word must not be "she" or "it," congratulate yourself. Different pupils having named the result of their thinking we have "and," "while," "for," "which", "intending," as connecting links which will properly join some new matter to the old.

The following is a series of composition lessons, the material being furnished in large part by a poem found elsewhere in the book—"The Corn Song."

1. A picture in words of the farmer's barn, on the floor of which the corn was heaped : its situation, size, color, various contents, inhabitants of all kinds —horses, cows, chickens, swallows.

Such a picture will draw upon a pupil's available stock of words, put to use his practical grammar, show his taste about barns and sentences, exercise his memory in bringing forward the materials, and his skill in putting them together.

2. A spring scene in the fourth and fifth stanzas, or suggested by them. The team plowing, nature of the soil, stumps of trees, the furrows, birds hunting breakfast. A day soon after, the planting, hot sun, a black cloud, thunder storm, scurry to the barn.

3. The corn field in July—a mass of green, the stalk, blades, ear, silk and tassel. How corn is cultivated; why cultivated. Some enemies of the growing corn. Pumpkin vines. Incident : the finding of an old scarecrow almost hidden in the tall corn, of no use now, looking forlorn enough.

4. The corn harvest, the shocks standing like rough tents, the field green with ragweed and bristling with the stubs, "the frost on the pumpkins." Incident · hauling home a load by the light of the full moon just above the eastern horizon, in the background the barn and the farmhouse, blue smoke curling from the chimney, a ruddy light shining from the kitchen window.

5. A winter scene—field all white except the brown or gray stubs of the cut corn stalks; a deep snowdrift along the fence ; some chickadees hopping about on the limbs of an oak which stands near the gate, hunting insects' eggs on the under side of the brown leaves ; a few shocks that have not been husked, the snow about them printed with tracks of field mice, squirrels, and birds.

6. The old mill—a trip to it on the sled with sacks of shelled corn to be ground into meal—a skate on the pond—a fire built of drift—cracking sounds in the ice.

In a school where the pupils' powers of observation are stimulated, and directed upon the great world which lies all around them, an excellent exercise in composition of the following type may be given. The home of the boys and girls, we will say, is in one of our central states. From their geography they have learned that there are parts of the earth where, at the sea level, ice never forms, either over the pond or in shining spears along the eaves, and snow never falls. Ask the class to think of a boy or a girl of their own age, in, say, one of the new schools of Cuba; to think of what he does not know about our winter; and to write him a series of three or four letters to tell him all about it. The subject will grow under their hands. They must think themselves into his place in order to write what he will comprehend; in recalling and arranging this material there is work for the memory and the taste, as also in selecting from their verbal stores the aptest words to express what they know. Of course, while doing this, they must consult neither geographies nor encyclopedias, which have so much to answer for in this era of " papers. "

An exercise analogous to the foregoing, but somewhat more difficult, would be to have the pupils transport themselves in imagination to the home of their correspondent, and answer their own letters from his point of view.

PART II.

SELECTED LESSONS FOR STUDY.

WHAT A BIRD TAUGHT.

1. Why do you come to my apple tree,
   Little bird so gray ?
   Twit-twit, twit-twit, twit-twit-twee
   That was all he would say.

2. Why do you lock your rosy feet
   So closely round the spray ?
   Twit-twit, twit-twit, twit-tweet !
   That was all he would say.

3. Where is your mate ? come, answer me,
   Little bird so gray.
   Twit-twit-twit ! twit-twit-twee !
   · That was all he would say.

4. This little wilding of the wood,
   With wing so gray and fleet,
   Did just the best for you he could,
   And that is why 't was sweet.

Alice Cary.

1. Can you give one reason why the little bird came ?
2. How does he hold on to his perch ? What is the "spray " ? Give another meaning for the word " spray."

47

3. Where do you think his mate was ? Hunting for food ? Sitting on her nest ? Can this little bird be a robin ? a goldfinch ? a song sparrow ?

4. What do you think this bird taught ?

THE KINGBIRD.

1. The kingbird is not bigger than a robin.

2. He eats flies, and worms, and bugs, and berries.

3. He builds his nest in a tree, near some house.

4. When there are young ones in the nest, he sits on the top of a tree near them.

5. He watches to see that no bird comes to hurt them or their mother.

6. If a hawk, a crow, or even an eagle comes near, he makes a dash at it.

7. Though he is so small, he is brave, and he is also very active.

8. He never fails to drive off other birds from his nest.

9. He flies around and around the eagle, and suddenly strikes him with his sharp bill.

10. He strikes at his eye, and then darts away before the eagle can catch him.

11. The eagle soon grows tired of this kind of a battle and flies away.

12. In the fall the kingbird, like the bluebird and the robin, flies away to the south where he can find plenty to eat.

Now that we have read this lesson about the kingbird, and have looked closely at his picture, let us close our books and talk about this little king in feathers.

1. How large is the kingbird ?

2. As he eats hundreds of gnats and flies, can you think of any reason for his sitting on a bare limb or on a fence post ?

4. What does he do when there are young ones in the nest ?

Can you tell the color of the tip of his tail ? his throat and breast ?

Why is he called " kingbird " ? sometimes " flycatcher " ? sometimes " bee-martin " ?

Once as I was driving near a tree, a large hawk flew out of the top and spread his wings for a sail across the field to the woods. Just as he started a kingbird darted at him and sat upon his back and had a fine ride. When they had almost reached the woods the kingbird shot off from his strange ship without saying good-bye or paying for his trip.

IF I WERE A SUNBEAM.

1. "If I were a sunbeam,
   I know what I'd do ;
   I would seek white lilies,
   Roaming woodlands through.

Read. and Comp.—4.

I would steal among them,
   Softest light I'd shed,
Until every lily
   Raised its drooping head.

2. "If I were a sunbeam,
   I know where I'd go ;
Into lowly hovels,
   Dark with want and woe :
Till sad hearts looked upward,
   I would shine and shine ;
Then they'd think of heaven,
   Their sweet home and mine.

1. Notice that "I'd" should not be emphasized. What are "woodlands"? Name several things you might find there. Would you stop near the edge of the woodland? What does "steal" mean in this poem? Give another meaning? What would the lily do when the sunbeam came?

2. Where else would the sunbeam go? Who live in these "lowly hovels"? Why were these hovels "dark"? What good would the sunbeam do there? Of what would it be a sign? What does the sunbeam call heaven?

THE BEAVER.

1. The beaver is found chiefly in North America. It is about three and a half feet long, including the flat paddle-shaped tail, which is a foot in length.

2. The long, shining hair on the back is chestnut-colored, while the fine, soft fur that lies next the skin is grayish brown.

3. Beavers build themselves most curious huts to live in, and quite frequently a great number of these

huts are placed close together, like the buildings in a town.

4. They always build their huts on the banks of rivers or lakes, for they swim much more easily than they walk, and prefer moving about in the water.

5. When they build on the bank of a running stream, they make a dam across the stream for the purpose of keeping the water at the height they wish.

6. These dams are made chiefly of mud, and stones and the branches of trees. They are sometimes six or seven hundred feet in length, and are so constructed that they look more like the work of man than of little dumb beasts.

7. Their huts are made of the same material as the dams, and are round in shape. The walls are very

thick, and the roofs are finished off with a thick layer of mud, sticks, and leaves.

8. They commence building their houses late in the summer, but do not get them finished before the early frosts. The freezing makes them tighter and stronger.

9. They obtain the wood for their dams and huts by gnawing through the branches of trees, and even through the trunks of small ones, with their sharp front teeth. They peel off the bark, and lay it up in store for winter food.

10. The fur of the beaver is highly prized. The men who hunt these animals are called trappers.

11. A gentleman once saw five young beavers playing. They would leap on the trunk of a tree that lay near a beaver dam, and would push one another off into the water.

12. He crept forward very cautiously, and was about to fire on the little creatures ; but their amusing tricks reminded him so much of some little children he knew at home, that he thought it would be inhuman to kill them. So he left them without even disturbing their play.

1. What is the meaning of " chiefly " ? Give the length of a beaver's body ?

2. What is the difference between hair and fur ?

4. Do they prefer to walk or to swim ?

5. Why do they build dams ?

6. What materials do they use for this purpose ? If you saw one would you think a little animal built it ?

8. What are " early frosts " ?

9. Why do beavers peel the bark off the trees ? Explain the expression " in store ".

10. Who " highly prize " the beaver's fur ? Why ?

12. Why did that man creep "cautiously"? Why did the tricks remind him of his children?

THE CHILDREN'S FLOWER.

Dear dandelion, you sunshiny thing,
How many toys for the young folks you bring;
Watch chains for Nanny, and trumpets for Ned,
Funny green curls for the baby's bald head
Next you're a weather-cock ready to show,
When your white seeds fly, which way the winds
    blow.
Friend of the barefoot boy, gold of the poor,
You're a wee playhouse at each child's door.

Selected.

1. Why is the dandelion called "the children's flower"? Why "sunshiny"? Name the "toys." What is a weather-cock? Why do the seeds fly so easily? Why is it called the "friend" of the barefoot boy? Would the thistle be called that? What is meant by "gold of the poor"?

HENRY AND THE BEE.

1. Henry went out into the woods one day to look for birds' nests. He did not want to harm the nests, but only to know where they were.

He already knew of one nest. It was a very pretty one, and there were four blue eggs in it when he first found it. He had not touched it, but he had peeped into it almost every day for three weeks; and now, in place of the eggs, there were four tiny birds.

2. These birds were odd-looking little creatures. They had big mouths, and kept them open for the worms which the old birds brought to them. They seemed to be always hungry. Henry thought it would

be pleasant to watch them till their wings were strong enough for them to fly away.

3. On the day of which I am telling you, Henry went farther into the woods than he had ever been before. He saw a great many birds, but he could not find any nests.

At last he stopped. He was very tired, and thought he would go back home. He looked around to find a path that would take him out of the woods. But there was no path of any kind. He did not know which way to go.

4. He sat down on a log and thought about it. How could he find his way home? Must he stay all night in the woods, without any light but that of the stars? Must he sleep on a bed of leaves?

He called as loudly as he could. But no one heard him. He saw a bird fly down to the brook to drink. The birds could find their way through the thick woods. But what was a little boy to do?

Would he have to stay there without any dinner? He was hungry now. If he had only brought some cakes with him!

5. While Henry was looking around and wondering what he should do, he heard a sound that he knew quite well. It was a low, buzzing song that he had often heard at home.

It came from among some wild flowers that grew by the side of the log where he was sitting. Did any one ever hear of flowers singing? Henry knew that the buzzing sound was made by a bee. But where did the bee come from?

6. Nobody but Henry's father kept bees. This bee had come from the hives in the garden at home. It

knew the way back. Henry watched the busy little worker until at last it rose and flew away.

But it flew very close to Henry's face when it started. Henry thought that it said, "It is time to go home. Follow me!" He had heard his father say, "Bees always fly in a straight line." So he followed after this bee as fast as he could run.

7. Soon he was out of the woods. His father's farm was before him. He could see the house and barn. He could see the row of beehives in the garden.

Just as he passed the garden he saw a bee fly into one of the hives. It may have been the same bee that he saw in the woods; but he could not tell.

His mother was at the door. She said, "Where have you been, Henry? I was afraid that you were lost in the woods." Henry said, " I was lost in the woods. But I met one of our bees, and he showed me the way home."

Baldwin's School Reading by Grades.

Let us have a little study of emphasis in connection with this story. Read it carefully and see whether you agree with me that the following words should be pronounced either with more force or in a higher key :

1. Henry, woods, birds', harm, were, already, one, pretty, eggs, touched, every, three, eggs, birds.

2. Odd, big, worms, always, watch.

3. Day, farther, ever, great, any, very, path, way.

4. Thought, how, all, woods, light, leaves, called, **heard,** brook, birds, boy, dinner, now, only, cakes.

5. Wondering, often, wild flowers, singing, bee, where.

6. Nobody, this, home, back, rose, face, time, home, father, straight, fast.

7. Soon, farm, house, barn, beehives, garden, bee, same, mother, where, lost, woods, was, home.

PRETTY IS THAT PRETTY DOES.

1. The spider wears a plain brown dress,
        And she is a steady spinner ;
    To see her, quiet as a mouse,
    Going about her silver house,
        You would never, never, never guess
        The way she gets her dinner.

2. She looks as if no thought of ill
        In all her life had stirred her ;
    But while she moves with careful tread,
    And while she spins her silken thread,
        She is planning, planning, planning still
        The way to do some murder.

3. My child, who reads this simple lay,
        With eyes down-dropt and tender,
    Remember the old proverb says
    That pretty is that pretty does,
        And that worth does not go nor stay
        For poverty nor splendor.

4. 'Tis not the house, and not the dress,
        That makes the saint or sinner.
    To see the spider sit and spin,
    Shut with her walls of silver in,
        You would never, never, never guess
        The way she gets her dinner.

Alice Cary.

1. What is the color of the spider ? What does she spin ?
Where does she get the stuff to spin ? Why is her web called
a " silver house " ? Is she not quieter than a mouse ?

2. How does she plan to do murder ?   Upon how many feet does she move " with careful tread ?"

3. What wise old saying is quoted ?

4. What is it that does make the saint or sinner ?

WHERE THERE IS A WILL THERE IS A WAY.

1. Henry Bond was about ten years old when his father died.   His mother found it difficult to provide for the support of a large family, thus left entirely in her care.   By good management, however, she contrived to do so, and also to send Henry, the oldest, to school, and to supply him, for the most part, with such books as he needed.

2. At one time, however, Henry wanted a grammar, in order to join a class in that study, and his mother could not furnish him with the money to buy it.   He was very much troubled about it, and went to bed with a heavy heart, thinking what could be done.

3. On waking in the morning, he found that a deep snow had fallen, and the cold wind was blowing furiously.   " Ah," said he, " it is an ill wind that blows nobody good."

4. He rose, ran to the house of a neighbor, and offered his service to clear a path around his premises. The offer was accepted.   Having completed this work, and received his pay, he went to another place for the same purpose, and then to another, until he had earned enough to buy a grammar.

5. When school commenced, Henry was in his seat, the happiest boy there, ready to begin the lesson in his new book.

1. After the first section is read aloud in class, the question may be asked whether Henry's mother was rich or

poor after the death of his father.   Having decided that she
was not rich, the class, or some member of it, may be asked
to give reasons for this opinion.   A clearer light upon the con-
tent of the second sentence and the force of the separate
words should be sought.   Let the words "thus," and "en-
tirely," be considered.   "She contrived to do so," do what?
how did she do so?   This will bring forward what "man-
agement" stands for, and "contrived."   Did she do it easily?
What did she do besides support the family?   Did she buy
all of Henry's books?   What shows that she did not?

2. This paragraph is much simpler than the preceding one.
What was Henry troubled about?   What did he do?   What
other expression shows that Henry was troubled?   Have the
class point out a word already used that would do instead of
"wanted" ; two instead of "furnish."   "At one time" is
rather indefinite ; and the last five words of the section add
nothing.

3. Here we have the time of year suggested, and an old
proverb is quoted whose application is to be found in para-
graph 4.

4. Perhaps some boy who has handled the shovel will think
it a poor time for path-making when a furious wind is drifting
the snow.   What was Henry's offer ?   Show that the offer was
agreed to.   "This work," what work ?   "Same purpose,"
what purpose ?   Name a word that will do instead of " prem-
ises ; " " completed."   Cause " accepted " and " receive " to
change places, and notice the damage done.

5. Would "began" be a better word than "commenced"? It
would were it not for " begin " on the next line.   How would
" opened " do ?   Give the reason of Henry's happiness.   Was
it in owning a grammar, thinking about the good he would
get from it, or because he had earned it himself ?   What had
Henry earned besides a grammar ?   What kind of a boy was
Henry ?

STRAWBERRIES.

1. Little Pearl Honeydew, six years old,
   From her bright ear parted the curls of gold ;
   And laid her head on the strawberry bed,
   To hear what the red-cheeked berries said.

2. Their cheeks were blushing, their breath was sweet,
   She could almost hear their little hearts beat ;
   And the tiniest, lisping, whispering sound
   That ever you heard, came up from the ground.

3. "Little friends," she said, "I wish I knew
   How it is you thrive on sun and dew !"
   And this is the story the berries told
   To little Pearl Honeydew, six years old.

4. "You wish you knew ? And so do we.
   But we can't tell you, unless it be
   That the same kind Power that cares for you
   Takes care of poor little berries, too.

5. "Tucked up snugly, and nestled below
   Our coverlid of wind-woven snow,
   We peep and listen, all winter long,
   For the first spring day and the bluebird's song.

6. "When the swallows fly home to the old brown
       shed,
   And the robins build on the bow overhead,
   Then out from the mold, from the darkness and
       cold,
   Blossom and runner and leaf unfold.

7. "Apple blooms whiten, and peach blooms fall,
　And roses are gay by the garden wall,
　Ere the daisy's dial gives the sign
　That we can invite little Pearl to dine.

8. "The days are longest, the month is June,
　The year is nearing its golden noon,
　The weather is fine, and our feast is spread
　With a green cloth and berries red."

J. T. Trowbridge.

1. Why did Pearl part the curls ?　What was the color of her hair ?

2. Why does the author say that the berries spoke in a tiny whisper ?

3. Upon what do the strawberries feed ?

4. What did little Pearl wish she knew ?

5. Is the red-cheeked berry "tucked up" under the coverlid ? For what do the strawberries listen besides the bluebird's song ?

6. At what time of the year do the swallows fly home and the robins build their nests ?

7. What color are strawberry blossoms ?　Apple blossoms ?　Peach blossoms ?　Do gardens now have walls around them ?　What is the "daisy's dial" ?

8. What time of the day is noon ?　Why is a certain day in June called the year's "golden noon" ?

THE FOX AND THE DUCKS.

1. On a summer day, a man sitting on the bank of a river, under the shade of some bushes, watched a flock of ducks on the stream.

2. Soon a branch with leaves came drifting among them, and they all took wing. After circling in the air for a little time, they settled down again on their feeding ground.

3. Soon another branch came drifting down among them, and again they took flight from the river ; but when they found the branch had drifted by and done them no harm, they flew down to the water as before.

4. After four or five branches had drifted by in this way, the ducks gave little heed to them. At length, they hardly tried to fly out of their way, even when the branches nearly touched them.

5. The man who had been watching all this, now began to wonder who had set these branches adrift. He looked up the stream, and spied a fox slyly watching the ducks. "What will he do next?" thought the man.

6. When the fox saw that the ducks were no longer afraid of the branches, he took a much larger branch than any he had yet used, and stretched himself upon

it so as to be almost hidden.   Then he set it afloat as he had the others.

7. Right among the flock drifted the sly old fox, and, making quick snaps to right and left, he seized two fine young ducks, and floated off with them.

8. The rest of the flock flew away in fright, and did not come back for a long time.

9. The fox must have had a fine dinner to pay him for his cunning, patient work.

1. What is the time of year ?   What signs in the picture show this ?   In the story ?

2. Why did the ducks fly away from the first branch ? Why did they not fly after more branches had drifted by ?

3. What is the meaning of " to drift "? " to float " ?

5. What made the man think that the branches were being sent down the river ?

Do you think that this story is true ?

SEPTEMBER.

1. The golden-rod is yellow,
    The corn is turning brown,
  The trees in apple orchards
    With fruit are bending down.

2. The gentian's bluest fringes
    Are curling in the sun,
  In dusky pods the milkweed
    Its hidden silk has spun.

3. The sedges flaunt their harvest
    In every meadow-nook,
  And asters by the brookside
    Make asters in the brook.

4. By all these lovely tokens
  September days are here,
  With summer's best of weather
  And autumn's best of cheer.
  Helen Hunt Jackson.

This little poem should be given to the children when "September days are here" in fact, and its statements can be made lifelike by comparison with reality. The most important thing is that the boys and girls enjoy it. It should be memorized, and pains should be taken to make its several statements clearly understood.

1. Note what part of the "corn" is meant, and why the limbs of the trees are bending more than they did weeks ago.

2. If the living gentian cannot be procured, pictures will help. The little folk, with pods in hand, might be called upon to explain "dusky," "silk," and "spun."

3. "Harvest" is sometimes a season of the year; a crop at others. Here it must be the head of the stalk of the sedge. "Asters in the brook," the teacher must make definite the difference between a shadow and a reflected image.

4. What "tokens" have been named? Why "lovely"? Tokens of what? "Cheer" perhaps, as used here, stands for good things to eat.

THE SQUIRREL'S ARITHMETIC.

1. High on the branch of a walnut tree
  A bright-eyed squirrel sat.
  Of what was he thinking so earnestly?
  And what was he looking at?

2. The forest was green around him,
  The sky all over his head;
  His nest was in a hollow limb,
  And his children snug in bed.

3. He was doing a problem o'er and o'er,
   Busily thinking was he ;
   How many nuts for this winter's store
   Could he hide in the hollow tree ?

4. He sat so still on a swaying bough
   You might have thought him asleep.
   Oh, no ! he was trying to reckon now
   The nuts the babies could eat.

5. Then suddenly he frisked about
   And down the tree he ran,
   " The best way to do, without a doubt,
   Is to gather all that I can."

Selected.

1. Name the four words that should be emphasized in this stanza.   In what stanza is the question of the third line answered ?

2. Why does the writer tell us these things ?

3. What is meant by " store " ?

4. What is a swaying bough ?   "Oh, no !" answers what ?

5. Why did he run down the tree ? Why are quotation marks used in the last two lines ?

THE VOICE OF THE GRASS.

1. Here I come, creeping, creeping everywhere ;
       By the dusty roadside,
       On the sunny hillside,
       Close by the noisy brook,
       In every shady nook,
   I come creeping, creeping everywhere.

2. Here I come, creeping, creeping everywhere ;
       All round the open door,
       Where sit the aged poor,

Here where the children play,
In the bright and merry May,
I come creeping, creeping everywhere.

3. Here I come, creeping, creeping everywhere;
    You cannot see me coming,
    Nor hear my low, sweet humming,
    For in the starry night,
    And the glad morning light,
I come quietly creeping everywhere.

Sarah Roberts.

1. Why is "creeping" a good word to tell what the grass is doing? Why is it repeated?

2. Point out the bad rhyme.

3. Why can you not "see" nor "hear"? Do not fail to emphasize "quietly."

Notice the contrast : sunny and shady, aged and children, night and light, noisy and quietly.

THE OLD EAGLE TREE.

1. IN a distant field, stood a large tulip tree, apparently of a century's growth, and one of the most gigantic. It looked like the father of the surrounding forest. A single tree of huge dimensions, standing all alone, is a sublime object.

2. On the top of this tree, an old eagle, commonly called the "Fishing Eagle," had built her nest every year, for many years, and, undisturbed, had raised her young. A remarkable place to choose, as she procured her food from the ocean, and this tree stood full ten miles from the seashore. It had long been known as the "Old Eagle Tree."

3. On a warm, sunny day, the workmen were hoeing corn in an adjoining field. At a certain hour of

the day, the old eagle was known to set off for the seaside, to gather food for her young. As she this day returned with a large fish in her claws, the workmen surrounded the tree, and, by yelling and hooting, and throwing stones, so scared the poor bird that she dropped her fish, and they carried it off in triumph.

4. The men soon dispersed, but Joseph sat down under a bush near by, to watch, and to bestow unavailing pity. The bird soon returned to her nest, without food. The eaglets at once set up a cry for food, so shrill, so clear, and so clamorous that the boy was greatly moved.

5. The parent bird seemed to try to soothe them; but their appetites were too keen, and it was all in vain. She then perched herself on a limb near them, and looked down into the nest in a manner that seemed to say, "I know not what to do next."

6. Her indecision was but momentary; again she poised herself, uttered one or two sharp notes, as if telling them to "lie still," balanced her body, spread her wings, and was away again for the sea.

7. Joseph was determined to see the result. His eye followed her till she grew small, smaller, a mere speck in the sky, and then disappeared. What boy has not thus watched the flight of the bird of his country!

8. She was gone nearly two hours, about double her usual time for a voyage, when she again returned, on a slow, weary wing, flying uncommonly low, in order to have a heavier atmosphere to sustain her, with another fish in her talons.

9. On nearing the field, she made a circuit round it, to see if her enemies were again there. Finding

the coast clear, she once more reached the tree, drooping, faint, and weary, and evidently nearly exhausted. Again the eaglets set up their cry, which was soon hushed by the distribution of a dinner, such as, save the cooking, a king might admire.

10. "Glorious bird!" cried the boy, "what a spirit! I will learn a lesson from thee to-day. I will never forget, hereafter, that when the spirit is determined it can do almost any thing."

Dr. John Todd.

1. How old do you think this tulip tree was? Notice all the places where the size of this tree is spoken of.

2. Why was this a strange place for this eagle to build her nest? Find out whether an eagle builds a new nest each year.

3. "Adjoining field," adjoining what? "returned," was returning; what is meant by "in triumph"?

4. Why did Joseph sit down under a bush? Why was his pity "unavailing"? How was he "greatly moved"?

5. What was "all in vain"? How was it shown to be in vain?

6. How long did the mother eagle study over the matter? Explain what is meant by "poised."

7. Tell what "the result" was.

8. Explain the expression "slow, weary wing."

9. What is meant by the "coast" being "clear"? What is the meaning of "save" and of "admire" as used here?

10. What was the lesson Joseph said he had learned?

How do we feel toward the workmen? toward Joseph? toward the mother eagle? toward the eaglets?

MY GHOST.

1. "Yes, Katie, I think you are very sweet,
    Now that the tangles are out of your hair,
  And you sing as well as the birds you meet,
    That are playing, like you, in the blossoms there.

But now you are coming to kiss me, you say :
    Well, what is it for ?   Shall I tie your shoe ?
Or loop up your sleeve in a prettier way ?
    Do I know about ghosts ?   Indeed I do.

2. " Have I seen one ?   Yes ; last evening, you know,
        We were taking a walk that you had to miss,
    (I think you were naughty, and cried to go,
        But, surely, you'll stay at home after this !)
    And, away in the twilight, lonesomely,
        (What is the twilight ?   It's getting late !)
    I was thinking of things that were sad to me !—
        There, hush ! you know nothing about them,
            Kate.

3. " Well, we had to go through the rocky lane,
        Close to that bridge where the water roars,
    By a still, red house, where the dark and rain
        Go in when they will at the open doors.
    And the moon, that had just waked up, looked
            through
        The broken old windows, and seemed afraid,
    And the wild bats flew, and the thistles grew
        Where once in the roses the children played.

4. " Just across the road by the cherry trees
        Some fallen white stones had been lying so long,
    Half hid in the grass, and under these
        There were people dead.   I could hear the song
    Of a very sleepy dove as I passed
        The graveyard near, and the cricket that cried ;
    And I look'd (ah ! the ghost is coming at last !)
        And something was walking at my side.

5. " It seemed to be wrapped in a great dark shawl
    (For the night was a little cold, you know);
It would not speak.   It was black and tall ;
    And it walked so proudly and very slow.
Then it mocked me everything I could do ;
    Now it caught at the lighting flies like me ;
Now it stopped where the elder blossoms grew ;
    Now it tore the thorns from a gray bent tree.

6. " Still it followed me under the yellow moon,
    Looking back to the graveyard now and then,
Where the winds were playing the night a tune—
    But, Kate, a ghost doesn't care for men,
And your papa couldn't have done it harm.
    Ah ! dark-eyed darling, what is it you see ?
There, you needn't hide in your dimpled arm—
    It was only my shadow that walked with me !"
                                        Mrs. S. M. B. Piatt.

1. What do you think Katie had been doing before she greets her mother in the first stanza ?

2. Are we told why Katie did not take a walk, too ?   Why will Katie "stay at home after this " ?   What was the little girl's question ?   What did her mother answer ?

3. Name three things which tell us where the walk led them. Why was that house "still " ? Explain " waked up," " afraid."

4. What was opposite the "still, red house " ?   Why does the writer put this neglected graveyard into her story ?   Do crickets " cry " ?   Why did not the author write "chirp " ? Do crickets sing ?   Do you know, when you hear it, the dove's song—*a-coo, coo, coo* ?   "The ghost is coming," that is, the ghost story is coming.

5. What signs of early summer in this stanza ?

6. What two things were needed to make the shadow ? Which way did the shadow point ?   How did Katie seem to

like the story ? For whose protection did she wish ? How
could she hide in her arm ?

OCTOBER'S BRIGHT BLUE WEATHER.

1. O, suns and skies and flowers of June,
   And clouds of June together,
   Ye cannot rival for one hour
   October's bright blue weather.

2. When loud the bumblebee makes haste,
   Belated, thriftless, vagrant,
   And golden-rod is dying fast,
   And lanes with grapes are fragrant ;

3. When gentians roll their fringes tight,
   To save them for the morning,
   And chestnuts fall from satin burs
   Without a word of warning ;

4. When on the ground red apples lie
   In piles, like jewels shining,
   And redder still, on old stone walls,
   Are leaves of woodbine twining ;

5. When all the lovely wayside things
   Their white-winged seeds are sowing,
   And in the fields still green and fair
   Late aftermaths are growing ;

6. When springs run low, and on the brooks,
   In idle golden freighting,
   Bright leaves sink noiseless in the hush
   Of woods for winter waiting ;

7. O, suns and skies and flowers of June,
    Count all your boasts together,
    Love loveth best of all the year
    October's bright blue weather.

Helen Hunt Jackson.

1. Does the writer of this little poem like June or October better ? What is it to " rival " ?

2. Why is the bumblebee called " belated " ? " thriftless " ? What is " loud " ? Where are the " grapes " ?

3. The fringed gentian closes with a sort of twist. " Satin burs," the inside of the bur. Why do they fall ?

4. Which are redder, the apples or the woodbine leaves ? Which will likely stay red the longer ?

5. Name one of those " wayside things." How does it sow its seeds ? The second crop of grass, or the ragweed that comes after the wheat is cut, is an " aftermath."

6. Why are the springs low ? What is the " freighting " on the brooks ? Why are the woods " hushed " ? For what are the woods waiting ?

THE SWALLOW'S NEST.

1. A swallow in the spring
    Came to our barn, and there beneath the eaves
    She tried to make a nest, and there did bring
    Wet earth and straw and leaves.

2. Day after day she toiled
    With patient art, but ere her work was crowned,
    Some sad mishap the tiny fabric spoiled,
    And dashed it to the ground.

3. She found the ruin wrought,
    But, not cast down, forth from the place she flew,
    And, with her mate, fresh earth and grasses brought
    And built her nest anew.

4. But scarcely had she placed
   The last soft feather on its ample floor,
When wicked hand, or chance, again laid waste,
   And wrought the ruin o'er.

5. But still her heart she kept,
   And toiled again ; and last night, hearing calls,
I looked—and lo ! three little swallows slept
   Within the earth-made walls.

Anonymous.

1. What time of year do birds build their nests ? This swallow is called the eave swallow. Why ? Why are these birds and the barn swallows called " masons " ?

2. What is meant by " crowned " ? " mishap " ? " fabric " ?

3. " Not cast down," what does that mean ?

4. Of what did these birds make their carpet ? Tell the fate of the second nest, the third nest.

5. Why does the writer say " and lo " ?   " Her heart she kept " means what ?   What is the nest called in the last stanza ?   What reward did the mother swallow have for her perseverance ?

HOW THE HORSE-CHESTNUT GOT ITS NAME.

1. There was a great noise out on the lawn. It seemed as if all the trees were trying to see which could make the most racket.

2. The old oak twisted his giant arms, and at last managed to make himself heard above the others while he told of his great age, and to what a good old family he belonged, and how through many centuries they had helped to make English homes beautiful.   He was going on to tell of their part in history, too, but before he had fairly begun the pine interrupted in a very rude way.

3. And with much moaning and tossing of her stately head, she said that her family was ever so much older, and that they had traveled farther, too, away from the cold Northland, where, even amid the ice and snow, they showed their glossy green needles. Their wood was used for ships, and in many lands the pines are loved very much by the children, because it is they who give them Christmas trees.

4. Then the elm, with stately grace, began her story. But she could only begin, because the horse-chestnut, who stood near her, made so much noise that one really could not hear anything else but—" You have all had a great deal to tell about your age and wisdom and many wonderful qualities. But I don't believe one of you can tell me how I got my name."

5. There was a lull for a full second, then a saucy young spruce exclaimed, " Pshaw ! any sapling can answer that. Give us something hard."

"I will hear your answer first," said Horse-Chestnut.

"Why, it's because your fruit is so much larger and coarser than ordinary chestnuts that it is called horse-chestnut in contempt," said young Spruce.

6. "I thought you didn't know," was the answer ; while two or three interrupted in concert, " Oh, no ! we knew better than that."

And Maple, who lived next to Horse-Chestnut and was very friendly with her, went on to explain : " It is because the nuts can be ground into meal that makes very good food for horses."

7. "Oh, Maple, have you lived next me all these years and never noticed, either ? If this gale coming my way will help me, I'll show you all."

So Horse-Chestnut tried to hold one small branch out stiff, the gale helped to snap it loose, and landed it right in Maple tree's arms.

" Now," said the Horse-Chestnut, "look at the little marks all along the bark.   What do they look like ?"

8. " Horseshoes !" answered every tree who stood near enough to see " There are just the right number of nails, and they show on the inside, too.   Here is the hoof, just like a real one, and this curve is like the horse's knee."

And if any of you " little folks " would see for your-selves, cut carefully about the curved marks on the bark of a horse-chestnut twig, and you, too, will find the horseshoe, the nails, and the " frog " which Mother Nature gave Horse-Chestnut tree.

Margaret P. Boyle.

This is a good story for reproduction. It should be read aloud to the class by two or three pupils in succession.   Then should follow a suitable exercise to test the attention and memory of the class.   The story should then be retold, each pupil putting it in his own words.

THE LANDING OF THE PILGRIM FATHERS IN NEW ENGLAND.

1. The breaking waves dashed high
    On a stern and rock-bound coast,
   And the woods against a stormy sky
    Their giant branches tossed ;

2. And the heavy night hung dark
    The hills and waters o'er,
   When a band of exiles moored their bark
    On the wild New England shore.

3. Not as the conqueror comes,
    They, the true-hearted, came ;
Not with the roll of the stirring drums,
    And the trumpet that sings of fame ;

4. Not as the flying come,
    In silence and in fear ;
They shook the depths of the desert gloom
    With their hymns of lofty cheer.

5. Amidst the storm they sang,
    And the stars heard, and the sea ;
And the sounding aisles of the dim woods rang
    To the anthem of the free !

Mrs. Hemans.

1. What one word will stand for "breaking waves"? Why did the woods toss their branches? Meaning of "against" the sky?

2. Does the sky seem lower on a dark night? What really hung over the hills and waters? What are "exiles"? Where had these come from? What is a "bark"? Why was it "moored"? When was the bark moored?

3. How does a conqueror come? How can a trumpet "sing"? What is fame"?

4. How do the flying come? What is the meaning of "flying" here? How did the pilgrims show their joy? What is "lofty cheer"?

5. What does the poet mean by "the stars heard"? "sounding aisles"? What kind of an "anthem" did they sing?

Name the different *sounds* of this poem.

Which stanza do you like best?

Why is there not a period at the end of the third stanza?

IN TIME'S SWING.

1. Father Time, your footsteps go
Lightly as the falling snow.
In your swing I'm sitting, see!
Push me softly; one, two, three,
Twelve times only. Like a sheet,
Spread the snow beneath my feet.
Singing merrily, let me swing
Out of winter into spring.

2. Swing me out, and swing me in!
Trees are bare, but birds begin
Twittering to the peeping leaves,
On the bough beneath the eaves.
Look!—one lilac bud I saw!
Icy hillsides feel the thaw.
April chased off March to-day;
Now I catch a glimpse of May.

3. Oh, the smell of sprouting grass!
In a blur the violets pass.
Whispering from the wildwood come
Mayflowers' breath and insects' hum.
Roses carpeting the ground;
Orioles warbling all around.
Swing me low, and swing me high,
To the warm clouds of July!

4. Slower now, for at my side
White pond lilies open wide.
Underneath the pine's tall spire
Cardinal blossoms burn like fire.

They are gone ; the golden-rod
Flashes from the dark green sod.
Crickets in the grass I hear ;
Asters light the fading year.

5. Slower still !   October weaves
Rainbows of the forest leaves.
Gentians fringed, like eyes of blue,
Glimmer out of sleety dew.
Winds through withered sedges hiss
Meadow green I sadly miss.
Oh, 'tis snowing, swing me fast,
While December shivers past !

6. Frosty-bearded Father Time,
Stop your footfall on the rime !.
Hard you push, your hand is rough ;
You have swung me long enough.
"Nay, no stopping," say you ? Well,
Some of your best stories tell,
While you swing me—gently, do !—
From the Old Year to the New.

Lucy Larcom.

1. How many syllables in each line ? How many feet ?
Notice the accents.   Why is Time called " Father " ? What
is meant by " sitting in Time's swing " ? Do we all sit in it ?
Why is the snow like a sheet ?   Why " twelve times " ?
Who is " singing merrily " ? Why " merrily " ?   What
likeness between Time's footsteps and the falling snowflakes ?

2. Why are the trees bare ? Why do the birds twitter ?
What are " peeping leaves " ? Where are they ? In which
direction do the hillsides slope which first " feel the thaw " ?
Name some birds that stay with us all winter ; some that go

away in the fall. On what day was "a glimpse of May" caught? What is a glimpse?

3. What feeling does this "Oh" express? Explain "blur," "pass," "whispering," "breath." Other names for the mayflower are trailing arbutus, and ground laurel. Which month is called the "month of roses"? Would it be so in Chile?

4. Why "slower"? Have you seen pond lilies? Where is the flower when it opens? Explain "spire," "burn," "flashes." What is the color of the cardinal blossom? What sound do the crickets make? The word "aster" means a star. Explain "light."

5. Explain "weaves," "rainbows." What are gentians like? Are not meadows green in October where you live? Why does the wind "hiss" when blowing through the withered weed stalks? What does this "Oh" stand for?

6. Why "frosty-bearded"? Explain "rime," "hand," "rough." What does the poet ask for? What is the reply? Does the swinging ever stop? Why does the swinging begin in the winter? Note in this poem the signs of the different seasons.

To get the best and fullest results from such a poem let the class compare it with some other, searching for points of likeness or unlikeness in words, meter, scene, spirit. For example, take Bryant's classic little hymn of praise to the fringed gentian.

TO THE FRINGED GENTIAN.

1. Thou blossom bright with autumn dew,
   And colored with the heaven's own blue,
   That openest when the quiet light
   Succeeds the keen and frosty night.

2. Thou comest not when violets lean
   O'er wandering brooks and springs unseen,
   Or columbines, in purple dressed,
   Nod o'er the ground-bird's hidden nest.

3. Thou waitest late and com'st alone,
   When woods are bare and birds are flown,
   And frosts and shortening days portend
   The aged year is near his end.

4. Then doth thy sweet and quiet eye
   Look through its fringes to the sky,
   Blue—blue—as if that sky let fall
   A flower from its cerulean wall.

5. I would that thus, when I shall see
   The hour of death draw near to me,
   Hope, blossoming within my heart,
   May look to heaven as I depart.

Each of these poems came from a heart full of love for
nature. There are few, if any, clear points of likeness. Let us
look for differences. The first poem is in the trochaic meter ;
the second is iambic. The one is rapid and noisy, the other is
slow and quiet. The one hurries through the year, glancing
at the signs of the shifting seasons ; the other steadily
regards an autumn blossom, casting only one lingering look
back to the violets and the nest-building ; the one is a formal
allegory in which are meanings partly hidden ; the language
of the other is literal, except a touch or two of personifica-
tion ; while the first has no moral lesson on the surface, the
second closes with a prayer.

BRANDYWINE FORD.

Gilbert Potter, whom we read about in the selections that
follow, is the hero of a novel called, " The Story of Kennett,"
written by Bayard Taylor.

For a long time Gilbert had worked hard and lived plainly
to earn and save enough money to pay off a debt, so that the
farm on which his mother and he lived should be entirely their
own. At last with the money in his saddlebags, one morn-

ing in November, he mounted his good horse, Roger, and rode away toward Chester where he expected to pay the debt and come home a free man.

The fall had been very pleasant, but the day of Gilbert's ride there was a great and sudden change in the weather. Instead of the warm sunshine glimmering through the hazy air, the rain came down heavily, not in drops but in sheets, and when Gilbert reached the river, the water was running swift and muddy, level with its banks.

His brave Roger carried him safely across, but not far beyond another enemy lay waiting for him. .

A robber, who bore the name of Sandy Flash, had for some months infested that region, causing people to look about them when they went from home after sundown, and to bolt their doors carefully before going to bed. This robber had heard of Gilbert's intended trip to Chester and what he would carry with him.

Gilbert had let the reins fall upon Roger's neck, and, wrapped in his wet cloak, was enduring the weather with a sort of grim patience, when, as the wise beast pressed close to a bank for shelter from the wind, a powerful hand gripped Gilbert by the collar and hurled him violently to the ground. We need not be told that the doer of this mischief was Sandy Flash, and that he soon had his hands in poor Gilbert's saddle-bags.

Gilbert did not go on to Chester, for he had no errand there now, but very sad and very sore he mounted his horse and turned his course toward home. It was late in the afternoon when he met his bad luck upon that dreary road. Night came early upon such a day—the " black, dreary night " which we are to spend with Gilbert in the story.

BRANDYWINE FORD.

I.

1. The black, dreary night seemed interminable. He could only guess, here and there, at a landmark,

and was forced to rely more upon Roger's instinct of the road than upon the guidance of his senses. Toward midnight, as he judged, by the solitary crow of a cock, the rain almost entirely ceased.

2. The wind began to blow sharp and keen, and the hard vault of the sky to lift a little. He fancied that the hills on his right had fallen away, and that the horizon was suddenly depressed towards the north. Roger's feet began to splash in constantly deepening water and presently a roar, distinct from that of the wind, filled the air.

3. It was the Brandywine. The stream had overflowed its broad meadow-bottoms, and was running high and fierce beyond its main channel. The turbid waters made a dim, dusky gleam around him; soon the fences disappeared, and the flood reached to his horse's body.

4. But he knew that the ford could be distinguished by the break in the fringe of timber; moreover, that the creek bank was a little higher than the meadows behind it, and so far, at least, he might venture. The ford was not more than twenty yards across, and he could trust Roger to swim that distance.

5. The faithful animal pressed bravely on, but Gilbert soon noticed that he seemed at fault. The swift water had forced him out of the road and he stopped from time to time, as if anxious and uneasy. The timber could now be discerned, only a short distance in advance, and in a few minutes they would gain the bank.

6. What was that? A strange, rustling, hissing sound, as of cattle trampling through dry reeds,—a sound which quivered and shook, even in the breath

of the hurrying wind. Roger snorted, stood still, and trembled in every limb; and a sensation of awe and terror struck a chill through Gilbert's heart. The sound drew swiftly nearer, and became a wild, seething roar, filling the whole breadth of the valley.

7. "The dam! the dam!" cried Gilbert, "the dam has given way!" He turned Roger's head, gave him the rein, struck, spurred, cheered, and shouted. The brave beast struggled through the impeding flood, but the advance wave of the coming inundation already touched his side. He staggered; a line of churning foam bore down upon them, the terrible roar was all around and over them, and horse and rider were whirled away.

8. What happened during the first few seconds, Gilbert could never distinctly recall. Now they were whelmed in the water, now riding its careering tide, torn through the tops of brushwood, jostled by floating logs and timbers of the dam, but always, as it seemed, remorselessly held in the heart of the tumult and the ruin.

9. He saw at last that they had fallen behind the furious onset of the flood, but Roger was still swimming with it, desperately throwing up his head from time to time, and snorting the water from his nostrils. All his efforts to gain a foothold failed; his strength was nearly spent, and unless some help should come in a few minutes it would come in vain. And in the darkness, and the rapidity with which they were borne along, how should help come?

10. All at once Roger's course stopped. He became an obstacle to the flood, which pressed him against some other obstacle below, and rushed over horse and

rider. Thrusting out his hand, Gilbert felt the rough bark of a tree. Leaning towards it, and clasping the log in his arms, he drew himself from the saddle, while Roger, freed from his burden, struggled into the current and instantly disappeared.

11. As nearly as Gilbert could ascertain, several timbers, thrown over each other, had lodged, probably upon a rocky islet in the stream, the uppermost one projecting slantingly out of the flood. It required all his strength to resist the current which sucked, and whirled, and tugged at his body, and to climb high enough to escape its force, without overbalancing his support. At last, though still half immerged, he found himself comparatively safe for a time, yet as far as ever from a final rescue.

12. Yet a new danger now assailed him, from the increasing cold. There was already a sting of frost, a breath of ice, in the wind. In another hour the sky was nearly swept bare of clouds, and he could note the lapse of the night by the sinking of the moon. But he was by this time hardly in a condition to note anything more.

1. Why did Gilbert have to "guess"? What were the landmarks? By Roger's instinct of the road is meant the horse's power to keep in the road though he could not see it. "His senses," whose? How did Gilbert know that it was about midnight?

2. Give the meaning of "vault," "fallen away," "depressed," "distinct."

3. Where is the Brandywine? What made the waters "turbid"? What caused the "gleam"? "Disappeared," were the fences moving?

4. What is the meaning of "distinguished"? Why was there a "break"? "So far," how far?

5. Explain "at fault," "discerned." Where was this timber?

6. What means "the sound drew nearer"? What caused this wild roar?

7. Explain "impeding." Do "flood" and "inundation" mean the same thing?

8. What is now taking place? Why "remorselessly"? What is meant by "heart"? What is the new word used for "noise"?

9. Explain "to gain a foothold." Why would help come "in vain"?

10. What made Roger an "obstacle"?

11. Were these timbers directly "over each other"? Could they so lie? Why did Gilbert not climb clear out of the water? Explain "projecting," "immerged," "comparatively."

12. What is the meaning of "assailed"? "a breath of ice"? "lapse"?

BRANDYWINE FORD.

II.

1. The moon was low in the west, and there was a pale glimmer of the coming dawn in the sky, when Gilbert Potter suddenly raised his head. Above the noise of the water and the whistle of the wind, he heard a familiar sound,—the shrill, sharp neigh of a horse. Lifting himself, with great exertion, to a sitting posture, he saw two men, on horseback, in the flooded meadow, a little below him. They stopped, seemed to consult, and presently drew nearer.

2. Gilbert tried to shout, but the muscles of his throat were stiff, and his lungs refused to act. The horse neighed again. This time there was no mis-

take; it was Roger that he heard! Voice came to him, and he cried aloud,—a hoarse, strange, unnatural cry.

The horsemen heard it, and rapidly pushed up the bank, until they reached a point directly opposite to him. The prospect of escape brought a thrill of life to his frame; he looked around and saw that the flood had indeed fallen.

3. "We have no rope," he heard one of the men say. "How shall we reach him?"

"There is no time to get one now" the other answered. "My horse is stronger than yours. I'll go into the creek just below, where it's broader and not so deep, and work my way up to him."

"But one horse can't carry both."

His will follow, be sure, when he sees me."

4. As the last speaker moved away, Gilbert saw a led horse plunging through the water beside the other. It was a difficult and dangerous undertaking. The horseman and the loose horse entered the main stream below, where its divided channel met and broadened, but it was still above the saddle-girths, and very swift.

5. Sometimes the animals plunged, losing their foothold; nevertheless, they gallantly breasted the current, and inch by inch worked their way to a point about six feet below Gilbert. It seemed impossible to approach nearer.

"Can you swim?" asked the man.

Gilbert shook his head. "Throw me the end of Roger's bridle!" he then cried.

6. The man unbuckled the bridle and threw it, keeping the end of the rein in his hand. Gilbert tried

to grasp it, but his hands were too numb. He managed, however, to get one arm and his head through the opening, and relaxed his hold on the log.

7. A plunge, and the man had him by the collar. He felt himself lifted by a strong arm and laid across Roger's saddle. With his failing strength and stiff limbs, it was no slight task to get into place; and the return, though less laborious to the horses, was equally dangerous, because Gilbert was scarcely able to support himself without help.

"You're safe now," said the man, when they reached the bank, "but it's a downright mercy of God that you're alive!"

8. The other horseman joined them, and they rode slowly across the flooded meadow. They had both thrown their cloaks around Gilbert, and carefully steadied him in the saddle, one on each side. He was too much exhausted to ask how they had found him, or whither they were taking him,—too numb for curiosity, almost for gratitude.

9. "Here's your savior!" said one of the men, patting Roger's shoulder. "It was through him that we found you. Do you wish to know how? Well— about three o'clock it was, maybe a little earlier, maybe a little later, my wife woke me up. 'Do you hear that?' she said.

10. "I listened and heard a horse in the lane before the door, neighing,—I can't tell you exactly how it was,—as though he would call up the house. It was rather queer, I thought, so I got up and looked out of the window, and it seemed to me he had a saddle on. He stamped, and pawed, and then he gave another neigh, and stamped again.

11. "Said I to my wife, 'There is something wrong here,' and I dressed and went out. When he saw me, he acted in the strangest way you ever saw ; thought I, if ever an animal wanted to speak, that animal does. When I tried to catch him, he shot off, ran down the lane a bit, and then came back acting as strangely as ever.

12. "I went into the house and woke up my brother, here, and we saddled our horses and started. Away went yours ahead, stopping every minute to look around and see if we followed. When we came to the water I rather hesitated ; but it was of no use ; the horse would have us go on and on, till we found you. I never heard of such a thing before, in all my life." Gilbert did not speak, but two large tears slowly gathered in his eyes, and rolled down his cheeks. The men saw his emotion, and respected it.

13. In the light of the cold, keen dawn, they reached a snug farmhouse, a mile from the Brandywine. The men lifted Gilbert from the saddle, and would have carried him immediately into the house, but he first leaned upon Roger's neck, took the faithful creature's head in his arms, and kissed him.

Bayard Taylor.

1. This first sentence tells us, if we think, whether the moon was new, or half, or full. What is meant by a "familiar sound"? The two men "*seemed* to consult." Why could not Gilbert be sure? "Drew nearer" to what?

2. "No mistake" about what? Explain "voice;" "pushed."

3. Why was it "not so deep"? Explain the expression "work my way."

4. Was there a "loose horse"?

5. What is it to "breast a current"?

6. Gilbert got his head through the opening in what? Explain "relaxed."

8. Why was he "too numb for curiosity"?

9. Does Gilbert here show any curiosity?

12. How did they respect "his emotion"?

LITTLE BELL.

1. Piped the blackbird on the beechwood spray :
   " Pretty maid, slow wandering this way,
       What's your name?" quoth he—
   " What's your name? Oh, stop and straight unfold,
   Pretty maid with showery curls of gold,—"
       " Little Bell," said she.

2. Little Bell sat down beneath the rocks—
   Tossed aside her gleaming, golden locks,—
       "Bonny bird!" quoth she,
   " Sing me your best song before I go."
   " Here's the very finest song I know,
       " Little Bell," said he.

3. And the blackbird piped ; you never heard
   Half so gay a song from any bird—
       Full of quips and wiles,
   Now so round and rich, now soft and slow,
   All for love of that sweet face below,
       Dimpled o'er with smiles.

4. And the while that bonny bird did pour
   His full heart freely o'er and o'er,
       'Neath the morning skies,
   In the little childish heart below
   All the sweetness seemed to grow and grow,
   And shine forth in the happy overflow
       From the blue, bright eyes.

5. Down the dell she tripped, and through the glade,
   Peeped the squirrel from the hazel shade,
       And from out the tree
   Swung and leaped and frolicked, void of fear,—
   While bold blackbird piped that all might hear,
       " Little Bell," piped he.

6. Little Bell sat down amid the fern—
   " Squirrel, squirrel, to your task return—
       Bring me nuts," quoth she.
   Up, away the frisky squirrel hies—
   Golden wood-lights glancing in his eyes—
       And adown the tree,
   Great ripe nuts, kissed brown by July sun,
   In the little lap dropped one by one—
   Hark, how blackbird pipes to see the fun !
       " Happy Bell," pipes he.

7. Little Bell looked up and down the glade—
   "Squirrel, squirrel, if you're not afraid,
       Come and share with me ! "
   Down came squirrel, eager for his fare,
   Down came bonny blackbird, I declare ;
   Little Bell gave each his honest share—
       Ah the merry three !
   And the while those frolic playmates twain
   Piped and frisked from bough to bough again,
       'Neath the morning skies,
   In the little childish heart below,
   All the sweetness seemed to grow and grow,
   And shine out in happy overflow
       From her blue, bright eyes.

8. By her snow-white cot at close of day,
   Knelt sweet Bell, with folded palms, to pray ;
        Very calm and clear
   Rose the praying voice, to where, unseen,
   In blue heaven, an angel shape serene
        Paused a while to hear.
   " What good child is this," the angel said,
   " That with happy heart, beside her bed,
        Prays so lovingly ? "
   Low and soft, O, very low and soft,
   Crooned the blackbird in the orchard croft,
        " Bell, dear Bell ! " crooned he.

9. " Whom God's creatures love," the angel fair
   Murmured, " God doth bless with angel's care ;
        Child, thy bed shall be
   Folded safe from harm ; love, deep and kind,
   Shall watch around and leave good gifts behind,
        Little Bell, for thee ! "
                                   Thomas Westwood.

1. " Piped," " No lark could pipe to skies so dull and
gray."—*Charles Kingsley.* " Spray," " O nightingale that
on yon bloomy spray warblest at eve."—*Milton.* " Showery
curls," a shower of curls. " Of gold," yellow.

2. " Beneath," at the foot of. " Gleaming," bright,
shining.

3. This is the English blackbird, a relative of the American
robin. " Quips and wiles," lively tunes. Why did he sing
so sweetly ? What effect did the singing have ?

5. What is a " dell ; " a " glade ; " " void."

6. " Task," what task ? What kind of nuts ? " Wood-
lights," probably the sun shining through the leaves. " July,"
earlier in England than in our country. " Fun," what fun ?

7. Who were invited to this party ? What is meant by "fare" ? "Twain," how many ?

8. "Crooned." "The catbirds have a way of crooning over their song in an undertone."—*Lowell.* "Croft," inclosure.

9. "Folded," angels shall care for it, like shepherds for the sheepfold.

This fine poem may well be studied in connection with the more familiar one, by Leigh Hunt, entitled "Abou Ben Adhem," in which Abou was blessed by God because he loved his fellow-men.

APRIL WEATHER.

1. Birds on the boughs before the buds
    Begin to burst in the spring,
Bending their heads to the April floods,
    Too much out of breath to sing !

2. They chirp, "Hey-day ! How the rain comes down
    Comrades cuddle together !
Cling to the bark so rough and brown,
    For this is April weather.

3. "Oh, the warm, beautiful, drenching rain !
    I don't mind it, do you ?
Soon will the sky be clear again, ·
    Smiling and fresh, and blue.

4. "Sweet and sparkling is every drop
    That slides from the soft, gray clouds ; '
Blossoms will blush to the very top
    Of the bare old trees in crowds.

5. "Oh, the warm, delicious, hopeful rain !
    Let us be glad together,
Summer comes flying in beauty again,
    Through the fitful April weather."

Celia Thaxter.

1. Notice the alliteration in the first stanza. Why are the birds out of breath ?

2. Why is the word " cuddle " particularly appropriate here ?

3. Why did the birds not mind the rain ?

4. Explain " slides," " blush," " bare." Name some trees of which this is true.

THE RAINBOW.

My heart leaps up when I behold
    A rainbow in the sky :
So was it when my life began ;
So is it now I am a man ;
So be it when I shall grow old,
    Or let me die !
The child is father of the man ;
And I could wish my days to be
Bound each to each by natural piety.
                    William Wordsworth.

The poet elsewhere records that as he grew older there did pass away a glory from the earth, but that there was a compensation in :

    A presence that disturbs me with the joy
    Of elevated thoughts ; a sense sublime
    Of something far more deeply interfused,
    Whose dwelling is the light of setting suns,
    And the round ocean, and the living air,
    And the blue sky, and in the mind of man.

DAFFODILS.

1. I wandered lonely as a cloud,
    That floats on high o'er vales and hills,
When all at once I saw a crowd,

A host, of golden daffodils ;
Beside the lake, beneath the trees,
Fluttering and dancing in the breeze.

2. Continuous as the stars that shine
    And twinkle on the milky way,
They stretched in never-ending line
    Along the margin of a bay :
Ten thousand saw I at a glance,
Tossing their heads in sprightly dance.

3. The waves beside them danced ; but they
    Outdid the sparkling waves in glee :
A poet could not but be gay,
    In such a jocund company :
I gazed,—and gazed,—but little thought
What wealth the show to me had brought :

4. For oft, when on my couch I lie
    In vacant or in pensive mood,
They flash upon that inward eye
    Which is the bliss of solitude ;
And then my heart with pleasure fills,
And dances with the daffodils.

William Wordsworth.

1. What excellent simile has the poet used to convey the idea of his complete loneliness ?

2. " Continuous," so close together as to give the eye the impression of a golden " way." " Ten thousand," did he count them ?

3. " Could not but," impossible not to be. What is the meaning of " jocund " ?

4. " What wealth " had the show brought ? " Vacant," thoughtless ; " pensive," thoughtful. " Inward eye," the

mind's eye which gives the power of seeing past images with all " the charm of visionary things."

Note the images called to mind by the poet : the slowly-moving cloud ; the splendor of the milky way ; the crowd of fluttering, dancing flowers ; the sparkling waves responsive to the wind.

Let the pupil try to tell what lesson this poem teaches.

THE CONCORD.

1. We stand now on the river's brink. It may well be called the Concord, the river of peace and quietness ; for it is certainly the most unexcitable and sluggish stream that ever loitered imperceptibly towards its eternity,—the sea. Positively, I had lived three weeks beside it before it grew quite clear to my perception which way the current flowed. It never has a vivacious aspect except when a northwestern breeze is vexing its surface on a sunshiny day. From the incurable indolence of its nature, the stream is happily incapable of becoming the slave of human ingenuity, as is the fate of so many a wild, free mountain torrent.

2. While all things else are compelled to subserve some useful purpose, it idles its sluggish life away in lazy liberty, without turning a solitary spindle or affording even water-power enough to grind the corn that grows upon its banks. The torpor of its movement allows it nowhere a bright, pebbly shore, nor so much as a narrow strip of glistening sand, in any part of its course.

3. It slumbers between broad prairies, kissing the long meadow grass, and bathes the overhanging boughs of elder bushes and willows, or the roots of

elms and ash trees and clumps of maples. Flags and rushes grow along its plashy shore; the yellow water lily spreads its broad, flat leaves on the margin; and the fragrant white pond lily abounds, generally selecting a position just so far from the river's brink that it cannot be grasped save at the hazard of plunging in.

4. It is a marvel whence this perfect flower derives its loveliness and perfume, springing as it does from the black mud over which the river sleeps, and where lurk the slimy eel and speckled frog and the mud turtle, whom continual washing cannot cleanse.

5. The reader must not, from any testimony of mine, contract a dislike towards our slumberous stream. In the light of a calm and golden sunset it becomes lovely beyond expression; the more lovely for the quietude that so well accords with the hour, when even the wind, after blustering all day long, usually hushes itself to rest. Each tree and rock, and every blade of grass, is distinctly imaged, and, however unsightly in reality, assumes ideal beauty in the reflection.

6. The minutest things of earth and the broad aspect of the firmament are pictured equally without effort and with the same felicity of success. All the sky glows downward at our feet; the rich clouds float through the unruffled bosom of the stream like heavenly thoughts through a peaceful heart. If we remember its tawny hue and the muddiness of its bed, let it be a symbol that the earthliest human soul has an infinite spiritual capacity and may contain the better world within its depths.

Nathaniel Hawthorne.

1. Draw attention to the fact that the text itself defines the word "concord." Note the composition of the phrase "most unexcitable," the effect of "most" extending over "sluggish"; the fitness of "loitered" to give us the rate of that slow-going river; as life is swallowed up in eternity, so the river in the sea. Look up in the dictionary any word of doubtful meaning, but notice that the connection defines "imperceptibly," "loitered," "vivacious," "incapable." How does the mountain torrent become a slave?

2. Why would a swift movement be likely to line the river with pebbles or sand?

3. What word in the first line conveys the idea of slowness? "Plashy," see this word in Bryant's lines "To a Waterfowl." Why does it seem that the water lily selects the position named?

4. State the "marvel." Why "lurk" rather than "live," or "stay"? Why the comma after "turtle"?

5. Where is the "testimony" referred to? Why should the reader not "contract," etc.? Meaning of "beyond expression"? Have you ever observed the fact about the wind here affirmed? Bring out the distinction between the *real* and the *ideal*. Why would you hang upon the wall a picture of something you would not allow in your yard?

6. What contrast? For what purpose? "Felicity of success," one picture as perfect as the other. Why "glows," "rich," "peaceful," "symbol"?

THE SANDPIPER.

1. Across the lonely beach we flit,
      One little sandpiper and I,
   And fast I gather, bit by bit,
      The scattered driftwood, bleached and dry.
   The wild waves reach their hands for it,
      The wild wind raves, the tide runs high,
   As up and down the beach we flit,—
      One little sandpiper and I.

2. Above our heads the sullen clouds
    Scud, black and swift, across the sky;
Like silent ghosts in misty shrouds
    Stand out the white lighthouses high.
Almost as far as eye can reach
    I see the close-reefed vessels fly,
As fast we flit across the beach,—
    One little sandpiper and I.

3. I watch him as he skims along,
    Uttering his sweet and mournful cry.
He starts not at my fitful song,
    Or flash of fluttering drapery.
He has no thought of any wrong,
    He scans me with a fearless eye;
Staunch friends are we, well tried and strong,
    The little sandpiper and I.

4. Comrade, where wilt thou be to-night,
    When the loosed storm breaks furiously?
My driftwood fire will burn so bright!
    To what warm shelter canst thou fly?
I do not fear for thee, though wroth
    The tempest rushes through the sky;
For are we not God's children both,
    Thou, little sandpiper, and I?

Celia Thaxter.

1. Why is the beach called lonely? What bleached the driftwood? "Hands," explain the use of this word in connection with waves. What is the force of " raves "?

2. "Sullen clouds," why so called? What caused them to "scud"? What are lighthouses? Color of those mentioned? Why were the vessels close-reefed? What sort of

Read. and Comp.—7.

motion does " flit " indicate ? What time of the day do you
think it was ?

3. Was the bird running ? walking ? flying ? Explain
" flash," " fluttering drapery," " any wrong," " staunch."

4. Who do you think the driftwood gatherer was ? Why
was she gathering wood ? What contrast between the woman
and the bird at night ? What likeness ? What is the lesson
of the poem ? Compare it with that of Bryant's lines " To a
Waterfowl."

THE RISING.

1. Out of the North the wild news came,
    Far flashing on its wings of flame,
    Swift as the boreal light which flies
    At midnight through the startled skies.

2. And there was tumult in the air,
        The fife's shrill note, the drum's loud beat,
    And through the wide land everywhere
        The answering tread of hurrying feet.
    While the first oath of Freedom's gun
    Came on the blast from Lexington.

3. And Concord roused, no longer tame,
    Forgot her old baptismal name,
    Made bare her patriot arm of power
    And swelled the discord of the hour.

                                   Thomas Buchanan Read.

1. Explain the words " North," " wild," " flashing,"
" boreal," " startled." " Wings of flame ", as if by signal
fires. Is the aurora seen only at midnight ?

2. Note the sounds that made up the " tumult." " Answer-
ing," " deep calleth unto deep."—*Bible.* " Oath." Is not this
a very forceful word for the report of a gun ?

3. How did Concord show that she " forgot " the meaning

of her name? "Made bare," got ready to use. Explain the expressions "arm of power," "discord of the hour."

How many feet to the verse or line in this poem? How many syllables to the foot? Which one is commonly accented? Notice that the first foot of several of the lines is a trochee, not an iambus, as "Out of," "Swift as."

THE SPACIOUS FIRMAMENT ON HIGH.

1. The spacious firmament on high,
   With all the blue ethereal sky,
   And spangled heavens, a shining frame,
   Their great Original proclaim.
   The unwearied sun, from day to day
   Does his Creator's power display;
   And publishes to every land
   The work of an almighty hand.

2. Soon as the evening shades prevail,
   The moon takes up the wondrous tale;
   And nightly, to the listening earth,
   Repeats the story of her birth:
   Whilst all the stars that round her burn,
   And all the planets, in their turn,
   Confirm the tidings as they roll,
   And spread the truth from pole to pole.

3. What though, in solemn silence, all
   Move round the dark terrestrial ball?
   What though no real voice nor sound
   Amidst their radiant orbs be found?
   In reason's ear they all rejoice,
   And utter forth a glorious voice,
   Forever singing as they shine,
   "The hand that made us is divine!"

Joseph Addison.

1. Explain use of "firmament," "spangled." In what other connection is this word frequently used? "Display," show; "publishes," makes known.

2. "Wondrous tale," story of her birth. Note the use of the word "burn," "Tidings," and "truth," the story of their birth.

3. "All," sun, moon, planets, stars. "A glorious voice,"
  "There's not the smallest orb which thou behold'st
  But in his motion like an angel sings."

—*Shakespeare.*

THE FIFTIETH BIRTHDAY OF AGASSIZ.

May 28, 1857.

1. It was fifty years ago
  In the pleasant month of May,
  In the beautiful Pays de Vaud,[1]
  A child in its cradle lay.

2. And Nature, the old nurse, took
  The child upon her knee,
  Saying: "Here is a story-book
  Thy Father has written for thee."

3. "Come, wander with me," she said,
  "Into regions yet untrod;
  And read what is still unread
  In the manuscripts of God."

4. And he wandered away and away
  With Nature, the dear old nurse,
  Who sang to him night and day
  The rhymes of the universe.

[1] Pä-ŏ deh vŏ.

5. And whenever the way seemed long,
    Or his heart began to fail,
She would sing a more wonderful song,
    Or tell a more marvelous tale.

6. So she keeps him still a child,
    And will not let him go,
Though at times his heart beats wild
    For the beautiful Pays de Vaud ;

7. Though at times he hears in his dreams
    The Ranz dez Vaches[1] of old,
And the rush of mountain streams
    From glaciers clear and cold ;

8. And the mother at home says "Hark !
    For his voice I listen and yearn ;
It is growing late and dark,
    And my boy does not return !"

Henry Wadsworth Longfellow.

1. Where and when was Agassiz born ?
2. What is this "story-book" ?
3. Explain the expression "regions yet untrod." "Manuscripts," handwriting.
4. Why do you think the poet says Nature "sang" ?
5. Explain "the way seemed long ; " "a more wonderful song."
6. Explain "still a child." "Go" where ?
7. Why does the poet speak of "glaciers" ?
8. "It is growing late," in the day ? in her life ?

THE MOUNTAIN AND THE SQUIRREL.

The mountain and the squirrel
Had a quarrel,
And the former called the latter "Little prig ;"

[1] Ron dā väsh.

Bun replied,
" You are doubtless very big,
But all sorts of things and weather
Must be taken in together
To make up a year
And a sphere.
And I count it no disgrace
To occupy my place.
And if I'm not so large as you,
You are not so small as I,
And not half so spry.
I'll not deny you make
A very pretty squirrel track.
Talents differ ; all is well and wisely put ;
If I cannot carry forests on my back,
Neither can you crack a nut."

Ralph Waldo Emerson.

Commit this poem to memory, drinking in the meaning of every line.

TO THE DANDELION.

1. Dear common flower, that growest beside the way,
   Fringing the dusty road with harmless gold,
       First pledge of blithesome May,
   Which children pluck, and, full of pride, uphold,

           Thou art more dear to me
   Than all the prouder summer-blooms may be.

2. Then think I of deep shadows on the grass,
   Of meadows where in sun the cattle graze ;
       Where, as the breezes pass,
   The gleaming rushes lean a thousand ways,
       Of leaves that slumber in a cloudy mass,

Or whiten in the wind, of waters blue
  That from a distance sparkle through
Some woodland gap, and of a sky above,
Where one white cloud like a stray lamb doth
  move.

3. My childhood's earliest thoughts are linked with
    thee ;
  The sight of thee brings back the robin's song,
    Who, from the dark old tree
  Beside the door, sang clearly all day long,
    And I, secure in childish piety,
  Listened as if I heard an angel sing
    With news from heaven, which he could bring
  Fresh every day to my untainted ears
  When birds and flowers and I were happy peers.

4. How like a prodigal doth nature seem,
    When thou, for all thy gold, so common art !
    Thou teachest me to deem
  More sacredly of every human heart,
    Since each reflects in joy its scanty gleam
  Of heaven, and could some wondrous secret show,
    Did we but pay the love we owe,
  And with a child's undoubting wisdom look
  On all these living pages of God's book.
                              James Russell Lowell.

1. Why the mention of " gold " ?   Why " harmless " ?
The love of real money is the root of all evil.   " Pledge " of
what ?   Can you think of any reason why it is " more dear " ?
Can you name a " prouder " flower ?
  2. What month is the poet thinking of in this second

stanza ? When would the leaves "slumber" ? Name two trees whose leaves would " whiten in the wind." What produces the change ? Why compare this white cloud to a stray lamb ? Do you think it a good comparison ? Have you ever seen a little white cloud that reminded you of a lamb ? Shelley, with this idea in mind, speaks of the clouds

> "Wandering in thick flocks along the mountains,
> Shepherded by the slow, unwilling wind."

3. Explain what " brings back the robin's song " means. What perches are robins likely to take when they sing ? "Secure in childish piety," with a child's undoubting faith. What does the poet mean by " untainted ears " ?

4. Why is nature like a " prodigal " ? John Burroughs, speaking of British wild flowers, says the bluebell in places makes the underwoods as blue as the sky, and that this is " one of the plants of which nature is very prodigal in Britain." " More sacredly," to think of every heart as a sacred thing. Each has a gleam of heaven which we could see were we to look into it as the child looks into the flower or listens to the bird. What do you think is meant by " living pages " ?

THE GLADNESS OF NATURE.

1. Is this a time to be cloudy and sad,
    When our mother Nature laughs around ;
When even the deep blue heavens look glad,
    And gladness breathes from the blossoming ground ?

2. There are notes of joy from the hangbird and wren,
    And the gossip of swallows through all the sky ;
The ground-squirrel gaily chirps by his den,
    And the wilding bee hums merrily by.

3. The clouds are at play in the azure space,
   And their shadows at play on the bright green
   vale,
   And here they stretch to the frolic chase,
   And there they roll on the easy gale.

4. There's a dance of leaves in that aspen bower,
   There's a titter of winds in that beechen tree,
   There's a smile on the fruit, and a smile on the
   flower,
   And a laugh from the brook that runs to the sea.

5. And look at the broad-faced sun, how he smiles
   On the dewy earth that smiles in his ray,
   On the leaping waters and gay young isles;
   Ay, look, and he'll smile thy gloom away.

William Cullen Bryant.

1. Why is a negative clearly the answer to the question?
"Cloudy," effect of the sadness upon the face. What time
of year do you think it is ?

2. "Hangbird," another name for the oriole.
"Gossip," is thought a fit term for the twittering sounds
of the swallow by such an authority as John Burroughs.

3. "Clouds," is it necessarily a cloudy day ? "Here,"
on the vale; "there," in the blue sky.

4. Note "titter," "smile," and "laugh," in one stanza.
Note the *sounds* of the poem: The joyful notes of the oriole
and of the wren, the "gossip" or twitter of the swallow as he
flies, the chipmunk's chirp or short, shrill cry, the hum of the
wild bee, the beech leaves tittering in the wind, the ever vary-
ing and always musical song of the brook.

Note things in motion : the swallows, the bee, the clouds,
the shadows, the aspen leaves swinging on their flat stems,
the beech tree in a lively rustle, the running brook, and the
leaping waters.

SOME OF LOWELL'S GARDEN ACQUAINTANCES.

1. A few years ago I was much interested in the house-building of a pair of summer yellow-birds. They had chosen a very pretty site near the top of a tall white lilac, within easy eyeshot of a chamber window. A very pleasant thing it was to see their little home growing with mutual help, to watch their industrious skill interrupted only by little flirts and snatches of endearment, frugally cut short by the common-sense of the tiny housewife. They had brought their work nearly to an end, and had already begun to line it with ferndown, the gathering of which demanded more distant journeys and longer absences. But, alas! the syringa, immemorial manor of the catbirds, was not more than twenty feet away, and these "giddy neighbors" had, as it appeared, been all along jealously watchful, though silent, witnesses of what they deemed an intrusion of squatters. No sooner were the pretty mates fairly gone for a new load of lining, than

" To their unguarded nest these weasel Scots
   Came stealing."

2. Silently they flew back and forth, each giving a vengeful dab at the nest in passing. They did not fall to and deliberately destroy it, for they might have been caught at their mischief. As it was, whenever the yellow-birds came back, their enemies were hidden in their own sight-proof bush. Several times their unconscious victims repaired damages ; but at length, after counsel taken together, they gave it up. Perhaps, like other unlettered folk, they came to the con-

clusion that the Devil was in it, and yielded to the invisible persecutions of witchcraft.

The robins, by constant attacks and annoyances, have succeeded in driving off the blue jays who used to build in our pines, their gay colors and quaint, noisy ways making them welcome and amusing neighbors.

3. Of late years the jays have visited us only at intervals ; and in winter their bright plumage, set off by the snow, and their cheerful cry, are especially welcome. They would have furnished Æsop with a fable, for the feathered crest in which they seem to take so much satisfaction is often their fatal snare. Country boys make a hole with their finger in the snow-crust just large enough to admit the jay's head, and, hollowing it out somewhat beneath, bait it with a few kernels of corn. The crest slips easily into the trap, but refuses to be pulled out again, and he who came to feast remains a prey.

4. Twice have the crow blackbirds attempted a settlement in my pines, and twice have the robins, who claim a right of preëmption, so successfully played the part of border ruffians as to drive them away,—to my great regret, for they are the best substitute we have for rooks. At Shady Hill they build by hundreds, and nothing can be more cheery than their creaking clatter (like a convention of old-fashioned tavern signs) as they gather at evening to debate in mass meeting their windy politics, or to gossip at their tent doors over the events of the day. Their port is grave, and their stalk across the turf as martial as that of a second-rate ghost in " Hamlet." They never meddled with my corn, so far as I could discover.

For a few years I had crows; but their nests are an irresistible bait for boys, and their settlement was broken up.

James Russell Lowell.

1. "Summer yellow-birds," yellow warblers, a bird usually mistaken for a "wild canary," or goldfinch. "Ferndown," probably consists of milk-weed fibres and down from the fronds of ferns. "Immemorial manor," the home of the cat-bird family for a length of time far beyond the memory of the present occupants. "Squatters," settlers without any legal claim to the soil. "To their unguarded," etc. This quotation is from "Henry V.," Act I., Sc. 2, and is as follows: "To her unguarded nest the weasel Scot comes sneaking."

2. "Unconscious victims," ignorant of the cause of their misfortune. "Unlettered," ignorant, without knowledge of books.

3. "Jays," are allied to the crows, but are smaller and more graceful. "Æsop," why do you think he is spoken of in connection with a fable? "Crow blackbirds," sometimes called grackles. Their dispositions are as gloomy as their plumage is dark. Life with them is a serious affair.

4. "Preëmption," the right of the first settler to buy before others. "Border ruffians," a reference to the people who came from Missouri or other slave states to settle in Kansas in the "late fifties." "Rooks," a family of the crow species.

> "Light thickens ; and the crow
> Makes wing to the rooky woods."

Shakespeare.

"Tent doors," near their nesting places. "Port," bearing, deportment. They do not run, or hop, but walk in a stately fashion. "Martial," "With martial stalk hath he gone by our watch."—"Hamlet," Act I., Scene 1. Explain "bait for boys."

THE HUSKERS.

(A few stanzas of this poem of Whittier's are here given as an introduction to the next lesson, " The Corn Song.")

1. It was late in mild October, and the long autumnal rain
    Had left the summer harvest-fields all green with grass again ;
    The first sharp frosts had fallen, leaving all the woodlands gay
    With the hues of summer's rainbow, or the meadow flowers of May.

2. Through a thin, dry mist, that morning, the sun rose broad and red,
    At first a rayless disk of fire, he brightened as he sped ;
    Yet even his noontide glory fell chastened and subdued,
    On the cornfields and the orchards and softly pictured wood.

3. And all that quiet afternoon, slow sloping to the night,
    He wove, with golden shuttle, the haze with yellow light ;
    Slanting through the painted beeches, he glorified the hill ;
    And, beneath it, pond and meadow lay brighter, greener still.

4. And shouting boys in woodland haunts caught glimpses of that sky,

Flecked by the many-tinted leaves, and laughed,
    they knew not why ;
And school girls, gay with aster flowers, beside the
    meadow brooks,
Mingled the glow of autumn with the sunshine of
    sweet looks.

5. From spire and barn looked westerly the patient
    weathercocks ;
  But even the birches on the hill stood motionless as
    rocks.
  No sound was in the woodlands, save the squirrel's
    dropping shell,
  And the yellow leaves among the boughs, low rust-
    ling as they fell.

We then read that while the harvest of the summer grains
was over, the corn crop stood ungathered, bleaching in the
sun ; and that in those fields the farmers were busy all day
long, pulling off the ears, hauling them to the barn, and piling
them in a great heap on the floor.

The sun went down, broad and red, as when he rose, and
just then in the east shone forth the milder glory of the moon.

Soon from many a farmhouse, the huskers were seen
coming. They gathered around that huge corn pile and began
their merry rustling task, lanterns swinging from pitch-
forks giving them all the light they needed. Upon the in-
vitation of the daughter of the farmer who was giving this
" husking bee, " the village schoolmaster sang " The Corn
Song " to a quaint old tune.

1. The poet gives the usual undue credit to Jack Frost as
a painter.

2. Can you mention anything in this stanza that is typical
of the season of the year ?

3. From what direction does the poet think of night coming ? What figure ? " Painted beeches," probably the brilliant effect of the sun on the beech leaves.

4. Perhaps the boys and girls had gone to the woods to search for nuts and flowers. Is the aster a favorite flower of the poets ? Can you name any other poem in which it is mentioned ?

5. Is there any reason why the weathercocks should look " westerly " ? What slight sounds render the silence more impressive ?

Notice that after " morning " and " glory " in the second stanza, and after " shuttle " in the third, a pause takes the place of a syllable. The time would be filled in if each of these words contained three syllables.

THE CORN SONG.

1. Heap high the farmer's wintry hoard !
    Heap high the golden corn !
No richer gift has Autumn poured
    From out her lavish horn !

2. Let other lands, exulting, glean
    The apple from the pine,
The orange from its glossy green,
    The cluster from the vine ;

3. We better love the hardy gift
    Our rugged vales bestow,
To cheer us when the storm shall drift
    Our harvest-fields with snow.

4. Through vales of grass and meads of flowers,
    Our plows their furrows made,
While on the hills the sun and showers
    Of changeful April played.

5. We dropped the seed o'er hill and plain
    Beneath the sun of May,
And frightened from our sprouting grain
    The robber crows away.

6. All through the long, bright days of June
    Its leaves grew green and fair,
And waved in hot midsummer's noon
    Its soft and yellow hair.

7. And now, with autumn's moonlit eves,
    Its harvest time has come ;
We pluck away the frosted leaves
    And bear the treasure home.

8. There, when the snows about us drift
    And winter winds are cold,
Fair hands the broken grain shall sift
    And knead its meal of gold.

9. Let vapid idlers loll in silk,
    Around their costly board ;
Give us the bowl of samp and milk,
    By homespun beauty poured !

10. Where'er the wide old kitchen hearth
    Sends up its smoky curls,
Who will not thank the kindly earth,
    And bless our farmer girls !

11. Then shame on all the proud and vain,
    Whose folly laughs to scorn
The blessing of our hardy grain,
    Our wealth of golden corn !

12. Let earth withhold her goodly root,
    Let mildew blight the rye,
Give to the worm the orchard's fruit,
    The wheat field to the fly :

13. But let the good old crop adorn
    The hills our fathers trod ;
Still let us, for his golden corn,
    Send up our thanks to God!

John Greenleaf Whittier.

1. "Wintry," is this adjective used in an ordinary or in a poetic sense ? Can you think of a word that would do instead of "lavish "?—overflowing ? wasteful ? abundant ? profuse ? "Horn," cornucopia, the horn of plenty, the emblem of abundance. "Her," why is Autumn feminine ? Would Winter be personified as masculine or feminine ? What other creatures besides man store away corn and nuts for winter ?

2. How could "lands exult"? What is the usual meaning of "glean"? Does the pineapple grow upon the pine ? The pineapple has its name from the general resemblance of its fruit to the pine cone.

3. "Better" than what ? "Hardy" means what ? "Cheer us," how ? Notice that winter is not personified.

4. "Changeful," what is the particular force of this adjective in connection with April ?

5. Would this stanza suit the latitude of Tennessee ? Do crows wait for the seed corn to sprout ? Why would not "scared " do as well as "frightened "?

6. What "waved "? What part of the stalk is called "hair"? What other name for "leaves "?

7. Does the moonlight on autumn evenings last longer than in summer or winter ? Wait and see, if you do not know.

8. "Sift," why is the broken grain sifted ? Can it be kneaded ? stirred ?

9. What is "samp "? "Homespun beauty," a beautiful

country girl simply dressed in cloth spun and woven at home.

" What hempen homespuns have we swaggering here ? "— " Midsummer Night's Dream," Act III., Sc. 1.

10. Must the hearth be " old " ? " Smoky curls," poetic form for curls of smoke.   Notice the difference in this use of the adjective and that in

> " And twinkled in the smoky light,
> The waters of the rill."

Do you know who wrote these lines ?   " Kindly," fruitful, beneficent.

11. " Proud and vain," those who mock the blessings of simple, healthful country life.

12. What is meant by the " goodly root " ? Is the potato a root.   Did the poet wish these things to happen ?

13. Explain " adorn."

TO A MOUNTAIN DAISY,

ON TURNING ONE DOWN WITH THE PLOW, IN APRIL, 1786.

> The dayesye or elles the eye of day,
> The emperice and flour of floures alle.
>
> *Chaucer.*

1. Wee, modest, crimson-tippèd flow'r,
    Thou's met me in an evil hour ;
    For I maun crush amang the stoure
       Thy slender stem.
    To spare thee now is past my pow'r,
       Thou bonnie gem.

2. Alas ! it's no thy neebor sweet,
    The bonnie lark, companion meet,
    Bending thee 'mang the dewy weet,
       Wi' spreckled breast,
    When upward springing, blithe, to greet
       The purpling east.

3. Cauld blew the bitter-biting north
   Upon thy early, humble birth;
   Yet cheerfully thou glinted forth
       Amid the storm,
   Scarce rear'd above the parent earth
       Thy tender form.

4. The flaunting flow'rs our gardens yield,
   High shelt'ring woods and wa's maun shield;
   But thou, beneath the random bield
       O' clod or stane,
   Adorns the histie stibble-field,
       Unseen, alane.

5. There, in thy scanty mantle clad,
   Thy snawie bosom sunward spread,
   Thou lifts thy unassuming head
       In humble guise;
   But now the share uptears thy bed,
       And low thou lies!

6. Such is the fate of simple Bard,
   On life's rough ocean luckless starr'd!
   Unskilful he to note the card
       Of prudent lore,
   Till billows rage, and gales blow hard,
       And whelm him o'er!

7. Such fate to suffering worth is giv'n,
   Who long with wants and woes has striv'n,
   By human pride or cunning driv'n
       To mis'ry's brink,
   Till wrench'd of ev'ry stay but Heav'n,
       He, ruin'd, sink!

8. Ev'n thou who mourn'st the Daisy's fate,
    That fate is thine,—no distant date;
Stern Ruin's plowshare drives, elate,
        Full on thy bloom,
Till crush'd beneath the furrow's weight,
        Shall be thy doom!

Robert Burns.

1. "Wee," small; "maun," must; "stoure," dust; "past," beyond; "bonnie," pretty; "gem," something small and precious.

2. "Neebor," neighbor; "meet," fit; "'mang," among; "weet," wet; "wi'," with; "spreckled," spotted.

3. "Cauld," cold; "glinted," shone.

4. "Flaunting," waving showily; "wa's," walls; "random," chance; "bield," shelter; "o'," of; "stane," stone; "histie," dry; "stibble," stubble; "alane," alone.

5. "Snawie," snowy; "guise," appearance; "share," plow.

6. "Starr'd," refers to guiding one's course by the stars, so our word "disastrous" means ill-starred; "card," the face of the mariner's compass; "lore," learning.

8. "Elate," exulting.

1. For what was it "an evil hour"?

2. Why does the poet call the lark the daisy's "neebor"?

3. "North," here means what? Define "cheerfully."

4. Why is the protection or bield said to be chance or "random"? What is stubble? When did this stubble grow?

5. Explain "scanty mantle." What colors does the Scotch daisy wear?

6. Note all the words that relate to the ocean.

7. "Such fate," explain; also "wrench'd of every stay"; would not "Heaven" have been a sufficient "stay" if clung to?

8. Who is spoken of? Is there anything to indicate his age? Who do you think is the subject of "shall be."

(The two stanzas following are excellent notes upon this poem.)

TO THE DAISY.

1. When Winter decks his few gray hairs,
   Thee in the scanty wreath he wears;
   Spring parts the clouds with softest airs,
       That she may sun thee;
   Whole summer fields are thine by right,
   And Autumn, melancholy wight!
   Doth in thy crimson head delight
       When rains are on thee.

William Wordsworth.

THE LARK.

2. To hear the lark begin his flight,
   And singing startle the dull night
   From his watchtower in the skies
   Till the dappled dawn doth rise;
   Then to come, in spite of sorrow,
   And at my window bid good morrow,
   Through the sweet-briar, or the vine,
   Or the twisted eglantine.

John Milton.

1. "Decks," adorns. Why "thinly"? Explain "few" and "gray," "thine by right." "Melancholy," sad,—"The melancholy days are come." "Wight," a person, generally used now in humorous writings. "Crimson," the daisy is prettier in bud than in the flower, as it then shows more crimson.

2. "To hear," what sound? "His watchtower," whose? "Dappled," spotted. Note the several things the lark does.

THE RAINDROP.

Once upon a time there lived away up in Cloudland some little water drops.

Their home was one of the most beautiful white clouds that rolled over the blue sky. But by-and-by their cloud house seemed to get larger and larger, and darker and darker, and one tiny little water drop whispered to the other in a frightened way, "What's the matter? Our house seems so dark, and it's getting large, and just look at all the new vapor coming into it! Why, you're getting bigger, too, and oh, dear, so am I. What can it all mean?"

Then the other little water drop laughed so hard it rolled over and over and almost fell out of the cloud window. Then it answered, "Why, dear, we're gathering our forces together and we're going to pour through the air and cut the biggest dash you ever heard of when we get down to earth.

"We fly through the air like fairies, and we can look down and see the people preparing for us. Some of them that are indoors run and shut down the windows. Then we fly at the window panes and make music on them; and sometimes we dash right into the house before they can get it shut up tight, for you know there are millions and millions of us, so we divide the work. One little drop couldn't do anything that you could see. We always find a great many people out of doors. It is such fun to catch them. A great many have forgotten their umbrellas too.

"Often the wind goes with us. But I wish he wouldn't, for he makes us appear so rough. The only creatures that really seem to enjoy being out while we're coming—are ducks. You know water rolls right off a duck's back."

"But tell me, as fast as you can, how we divide work," said the first timid little water drop. "It must be almost time to start, for this cloud is packed so full I'm sure not another one can get in." "Oh," said the other, "we go wherever we're sent—some of us fall right into the ocean and help push along great steamers,—some of us fall into rivers and streams and do work there for a while, then move on to the ocean later,—some of us sink into the poor, parched earth and give it new life,—some of us change into vapor and come up to Cloudland, and some of us refresh the flowers, and that is the very sweetest work of all."

Just then the signal was given that two clouds were meeting. A rush, a flash, a crash and the water drops were flying through the air,—some to do great deeds—some to water the tiny little spring violets.

The children saw it all, so they sang :—

> " Good morning to the friendly clouds
>   That bring refreshing rain
> Which patters out, ' Good morning, dears,'
>   Against the window pane.
> Good morning to the glad new day
>   Whate'er the skies let fall,
> If storm or sunshine, it is sent,
>   A loving gift to all."
>
> *Mary R. M. Harbison.*

Read this selection two or three times, and then try to write it in your own words.

EVENING AT GRAND-PRÉ.

1. Now recommenced the reign of rest and affection and stillness.
   Day with its burden and heat had departed, and twilight descending
   Brought back the evening star to the sky, and the herds to the homestead.
   Pawing the ground they came, and resting their necks on each other,
   And with their nostrils distended inhaling the freshness of evening.
2. Foremost, bearing the bell, Evangeline's beautiful heifer,
   Proud of her snow-white hide, and the ribbon that waved from her collar,
   Quietly paced and slow, as if conscious of human affection.
3. Then came the shepherd back with his bleating flocks from the seaside,
   Where was their favorite pasture. Behind them followed the watchdog,
   Patient, full of importance, and grand in the pride of his instinct,
   Walking from side to side with a lordly air, and superbly
   Waving his bushy tail, and urging forward the stragglers ;
   Regent of flocks was he when the shepherd slept ; their protector,
   When from the forest at night, through the starry silence the wolves howled.

Late, with the rising moon, returned the wains
from the marshes,
Laden with briny hay that filled the air with its
odor.

4. Patiently stood the cows meanwhile, and yielded
their udders
Unto the milkmaid's hand; whilst loud and in
regular cadence
Into the sounding pails the foaming streamlets
descended.
Lowing of cattle and peals of laughter were heard
in the farm-yard,
Echoed back by the barns. Anon they sank into
stillness;
Heavily closed, with a jarring sound, the valves of
the barn doors,
Rattled the wooden bars, and all for a season was
silent.

Henry Wadsworth Longfellow.

The above selection is from "Evangeline," one of the finest
pastoral poems in English. It would be well for teacher and
class to read and reread aloud the entire poem; carefully bring-
ing out the music of its rhythm. Longfellow painted most of
his picture of Grand-Pré from "copy" in his own beauty-
loving soul. Travelers tell us that there are no murmuring
pines and hemlocks there, but that the apple and willow
are kings among the trees. In the poem at stated seasons the
flood-gates opened, and welcomed the sea to wander over the
meadows, but Frank Bolles says · "To flood Grand-Pré with
salt water would be to carry ruin and desolation to its fertile
acres, and sorrow to the hearts of its thrifty owners."

1. "Now," when ? Give full time to the first syllable of each
line. "Twilight," what is it ? Does it descend ? "Brought

back," in what sense ? " Evening star," probably the planet
Venus, or Jupiter, or Mars. "Freshness," what was inhaled ?
Why fresh ?

2. What caused the heifer to walk quietly?

3. "Flocks," of what ? How did the watchdog show his
patience ? his sense of importance ? " Superbly," haughtily.
Note whether the latter word would fit into the line in place of
" superbly." " Protector," from what ? " Starry silence,"
how still it must be when the stars are the only noise-makers !
" Briny hay," from grass growing in the salt marshes.

Notice the country sounds : falling of the milk, the merry
echoes, the bang of the barn doors, the rattle of the bars.
Some essayist has said that this is the first echo of this last-
named sound in literature.

THE ENGLISH SKYLARK.

1. Take it in all, no bird in either hemisphere equals
the English lark in heart or voice, for both unite to
make it the sweetest, the happiest, the welcomest singer
that was ever winged, like the high angels of God's
love.   It is the living ecstasy of joy when it mounts
up into its " glorious privacy of light."

2. On earth it is timid, silent, and bashful, as if
not at home, and not sure of its right to be there at
all.   It is rather homely withal, having nothing in
feather, feature, or form to attract notice.   It is
seemingly made to be heard, not seen, reversing the
old axiom addressed to children when getting noisy.

3. Its mission is music, and it floods a thousand acres
of the blue sky with it several times a day.   Out of
that palpitating speck of living joy there wells forth
a sea of twittering ecstasy upon the morning and the
evening air.   It does not ascend by gyrations, like

the eagle and birds of prey. It mounts up like a human aspiration.

4. It seems to spread its wings and to be lifted straight upwards out of sight by the afflatus of its own happy heart. To pour out this in undulating rivulets of rhapsody, is apparently the only motive of its ascension. This it is that has made it so loved of all generations.

5. It is the singing angel of man's nearest heaven, whose vital breath is music. Its sweet warbling is only the metrical palpitation of its life of joy. It goes up over the roof-trees of the rural hamlet on the wings of its song, as if to train the human soul to trial flights heavenward.

6. Never did the Creator put a voice of such volume into so small a living thing. It is a marvel—almost a miracle. In a still hour you can hear it at nearly a mile's distance. When its form is lost in the hazy lace work of the sun's rays above, it pours down upon you all the thrilling semitones of its song as distinctly as if it were warbling to you in your window.

Elihu Burritt.

1 "In all," a shortening of the common phrase "all in all." "Root and all and all in all."—*Tennyson.* What is meant by "In either hemisphere"?

2. Give the meaning of "homely." Notice the alliteration, "feather, feature, form." Repeat the old "axiom."

3. Explain "mission," "floods," "sea." "Speck," Emerson calls our chickadee an "atom," and Keyser's kinglet is a "dot in feathers." How does it ascend? Do not reply, "like a human aspiration."

4. What does the lark pour out in rivulets? Shelley says the skylark pours its "full heart in profuse strains of unpremeditated art."

5. What is meant by "man's nearest heaven"? What are the angels in that heaven? Their joy turns to what? For what purpose may we think it mounts heavenward? Goldsmith praises the good preacher who

" Allured to brighter worlds and led the way."

6. Distinguish between a "marvel" and a "miracle." The lark of which Milton wrote, would sing from his watchtower in the sky so as to startle dull night away.

TO A SKYLARK.

(In connection with the study of the preceding prose selection, read very carefully these stanzas of a hymn which Wordsworth sang to the skylark.)

1. Ethereal minstrel! pilgrim of the sky!
   Dost thou despise the earth where cares abound?
   Or, while the wings aspire, are heart and eye
   Both with thy nest upon the dewy ground?
   Thy nest which thou canst drop into at will
   Those quivering wings composed, that music still!

2. To the last point of vision, and beyond,
   Mount, daring warbler!—that love-prompted strain,
   ('Twixt thee and thine a never-failing bond)
   Thrills not the less the bosom of the plain.
   Yet might'st thou seem, proud privilege! to sing
   All independent of the leafy spring.

3. Leave to the nightingale her shady wood;
   A privacy of glorious light is thine,
   Whence thou dost pour upon the world a flood
   Of harmony, with instinct more divine;
   Type of the wise who soar, but never roam;
   True to the kindred points of heaven and home!

Why call one of these selections prose, the other poetry ?
What is the main thought of the second piece not found in the
first ?   What beauty in the first is not found in the second ?
Compare the two, seeking points of likeness and unlike-
ness.

THE SNOWSTORM.

1. Announced by all the trumpets of the sky,
   Arrives the snow, and, driving o'er the fields,
   Seems nowhere to alight : the whited air
   Hides hills and woods, the river, and the heaven,
   And veils the farmhouse at the garden's end.
   The sled and traveller stopped, the courier's feet
   Delayed, all friends shut out, the housemates sit
   Around the radiant fireplace, enclosed
   In a tumultuous privacy of storm.

2. Come see the north wind's masonry.
   Out of an unseen quarry evermore
   Furnished with tile, the fierce artificer
   Curves his white bastions with projected roof
   Round every windward stake, or tree, or door.
   Speeding, the myriad-handed, his wild work,
   So fanciful, so savage, naught cares he
   For number or proportion.

3.   Mockingly
   On coop or kennel he hangs Parian wreaths ;
   A swan-like form invests the hidden thorn ;
   Fills up the farmer's lane from wall to wall,
   Maugre the farmer's sighs ; and at the gate
   A tapering turret overtops the work.
   And when his hours are numbered, and the world
   Is all his own, retiring, as he were not,

Leaves, when the sun appears, astonished Art
To mimic in slow structures, stone by stone,
Built in an age, the mad wind's night-work,
The frolic architecture of the snow.

Ralph Waldo Emerson.

1. The storm king sends forward his heralds to announce his coming. What are his heralds ? " Nowhere," a common and beautiful phenomenon. " Whited air," snow in the air. " Stopped," kept away. What word below shows that " delayed " and " shut out " are passive ? " Fireplace," why not stove, register, or radiator ? " Tumultuous privacy," is this use of the word similar to the skylark's " privacy of glorious light " ?

2. Come see the masonry as shown in the word picture. Where is this " quarry " ? Who or what is " furnished with tile " ? " Fierce," rude, cold. " Projected," the cornice of snow so often seen along the edge of a bank. " Myriad-handed," working in countless places at once. " Wild," defined in the context.

3. " Mockingly," placing such dainty ornaments on structures so homely. " Parian wreaths," no marble from Paros could equal the snow in whiteness and purity. " Swan-like," the thorn bush covered with snow looks like a swan. " Maugre," in spite of the farmer's sighs, the snow continues its work. " Hours are numbered," the time nature allowed him has expired. " World is all his own," everything is covered with his work. " Mimic in slow structures," what the wild storm wind, as a builder, can accomplish in a night, art, laying stone by stone, would require an age to reproduce.

THE KAATSKILLS.

1. The scenery of these mountains is in the highest degree wild and romantic. Here are rocky precipices mantled with primeval forests ; deep gorges walled in

by beetling cliffs, with torrents tumbling as it were from the sky.

2. The Kaatskills form an advance post of the great Appalachian system which sweeps through the interior of our continent, belting the whole of our original confederacy, and rivaling our great system of lakes in extent and grandeur. In many of its vast ranges, nature still reigns in indomitable wildness.

3. Here are locked up mighty forests that have never been invaded by the ax ; deep umbrageous valleys where the virgin soil has never been outraged by the plow ; bright streams flowing in untasked idleness, unburdened by commerce, unchecked by the milldam. This mountain zone is in fact the great poetical region of our country ; resisting, like the tribes that once inhabited it, the training hand of cultivation ; and maintaining a hallowed ground for fancy and the muses. It is a magnificent and all-pervading feature that might have given our country a name, and a poetical one, had not the all-controlling powers of commonplace determined otherwise.

4. The detached position of the Kaatskills, overlooking a wide lowland region, with the majestic Hudson rolling through it, has given them a distinct character, and rendered them at all times a rallying point for romance and fable. To me they have ever been a fairy region. I speak, however, from early impressions, made in the happy days of boyhood, when all the world had a tinge of fairyland.

5. I shall never forget my first view of these mountains. It was in the course of a voyage up the Hudson, in the good old times before steamboats and railroads had driven all poetry and romance out of

travel. A voyage up the Hudson in those days was
equal to a voyage to Europe at present, and cost al-
most as much time. I was a lively boy, of easy faith,
and prone to relish everything that partook of the
marvelous.

6. Among the passengers on board the sloop was a
veteran Indian trader, on his way to the lakes to traf-
fic with the natives. He had discovered my propen-
sity, and amused himself by telling Indian legends
and grotesque stories about every noted place on the
river.

7. We were all day slowly tiding along in sight of
the Kaatskills, so that he had full time to weave his
narratives and dole them out to me as I lay on the
deck, gazing upon these mountains and wondering at
their ever-changing shapes and hues. Sometimes
they seemed to approach, at others to recede ; during
the heat of the day they almost melted into a sultry
haze ; as the day declined they deepened in tone ; their
summits were brightened by the last rays of the sun,
and later in the evening their whole outline was
printed in deep purple against an amber sky.

Arranged from Washington Irving.

1. Of what does this scenery consist ?   " Romantic," wildly
picturesque. " Mantled," concealed. " Primeval," belonging
to the first ages. " Here stands the forest primeval."—*Long-
fellow.* " Beetling," overhanging. " From the sky," where
does the observer stand ?

2. " Advance post," compared to what ? " Confederacy,"
the thirteen colonies. " Rivaling," having equal claims.
" Grandeur " always implies what ? " Indomitable," untama-
ble.

3. " Invaded," no trees have been cut down.   " Umbrage-

ous," heavily shaded. "Virgin," here means untilled. "Untasked," having no work to do. "Unburdened," free from boats loaded with produce. "Poetical region," one whose beauty would make a fit subject for a poet. "Commonplace," can you explain what is meant by this word?

4. Detached," verify this statement by looking at the map. "Rallying point," favorite subject.

5. How can steamboats and railroads "drive out poetry"? Did Irving ever make the voyage to Europe? Tell in your own words the kind of boy Irving says he was.

6. What do you suppose this trader got from the Indians? "Grotesque," wild, fantastic, odd.

7. "Tiding," going up with the tide. "Weave," out of what? "Dole," tell one by one. "Tone," color; "printed," like the figure of the waterfowl in Bryant's poem.

THE THUNDERSTORM.

1. In the second day of the voyage they came to the Highlands. It was the latter part of a calm, sultry day, that they floated gently with the tide between these stern mountains. There was that perfect quiet which prevails over nature in the languor of summer heat; the turning of a plank, or the accidental falling of an oar on deck, was echoed from the mountain side and reverberated along the shores; and, if by chance the captain gave a shout of command, there were airy tongues which mocked it from every cliff.

2. Dolph gazed about him in mute delight and wonder at these scenes of nature's magnificence. To the left the Dunderberg reared its woody precipices, height over height, forest over forest, away into the deep summer sky. To the right, strutted forth the bold promontory of Antony's Nose, with a solitary eagle wheeling about it; while beyond, mountain succeeded

Read. and Comp.—9.

to mountain, until they seemed to lock their arms together, and confine this mighty river in their embraces.

3. In the midst of his admiration, Dolph remarked a pile of bright snowy clouds peering above the western heights. It was succeeded by another, and another, each seemingly pushing onward its predecessor, and towering, with dazzling brilliancy, in the deep blue atmosphere; and now muttering peals of thunder were faintly heard rolling behind the mountains. The river, hitherto still and glassy, reflecting pictures of the sky and land, now showed a dark ripple at a distance, as the wind came creeping up it. The fishhawks wheeled and screamed, and sought their nests on the high, dry trees; the crows flew clamorously to the crevices of the rocks; and all nature seemed conscious of the approaching thunder gust.

4. The clouds now rolled in volumes over the mountain tops; their summits still bright and snowy, but the lower parts of an inky blackness. The rain began to patter down in broad and scattered drops; the wind freshened and curled up the waves; at length it seemed as if the bellying clouds were torn open by the mountain tops, and complete torrents of rain came rattling down. The lightning leaped from cloud to cloud, and streamed quivering against the rocks, splitting and rending the stoutest forest trees. The thunder burst in tremendous explosions; the peals were echoed from mountain to mountain; they crashed upon Dunderberg, and then rolled up the long defile of the highlands, each headland making a new echo, until old Bull Hill seemed to bellow back the storm.

5. For a time the scudding rack and mist and the

sheeted rain almost hid the landscape from the sight.
There was a fearful gloom, illumined still more fear-
fully by the streams of lightning which glittered
among the raindrops. Never had Dolph beheld such
an absolute warring of the elements ; it seemed as if
the storm was tearing and rending its way through
this mountain defile, and had brought all the artillery
of heaven into action.

Washington Irving.

1. Note that the vessel floats with the tide up the river,
and think of the reason. Do the words "the turning of a
plank" add more to the picture than "every slight noise"
would have done ? Why ? Why not have "accidental"
describe both the turning of a plank and the falling of an oar ?
"Reverberated." We praise our language for its wealth of
short words, and for most purposes it is a mark of good taste
to use these rather than the "long-tailed words in *osity* and
ation," but there is a time for the thundering polysylla-
ble. In "reverberated" we can almost hear the reëchoing
for which it stands. "Airy tongues" are only other "rever-
berations." Viola in "Twelfth Night" calls echo "the bab-
bling gossip of the air." In "Comus" Milton wrote :

> —"A thousand fantasies
> Begin to throng into my memory,
> Of calling shapes, and beck'ning shadows dire,
> And airy tongues, that syllable men's names
> On sands, and shores, and desert wildernesses."

2. The presence of an observer idling on the deck, mute
with delight and wonder, seeing with his bodily eye the things
which our fancy is striving to paint for us, lends a human
interest to the scene. We sympathize with Dolph's admiring
wonder, our pleasure is a copy of his. "Forest over forest"
recalls Goldsmith's, "Woods over woods." "The deep sum-
mer sky" pleases the ear and the fancy. "Deep,"

Byron wrote · "The cold, white moon looks deeply down."
"Strutted," note that the promontory did not seem to sail
like a ship, nor glide "like shadows over streams," nor "swim
into his ken" like a "new planet." Give one reason why
you think the word well-chosen. Why does the writer of
the story send but one eagle to fly around this peak ? A recol-
lection of some experience of his own ? "Solitary," a good
coloring word in the picture. Are eagles likely to be found
in flocks ? "Wheeling," circling. "Succeeded," passed in
procession ; came into view one after another, filling the space
in front.

3. "Admiration," wonder and pleasure ; "remarked,"
noticed. "Thunder," perhaps Rip Van Winkle's friends
playing at nine-pins. "Pictures of the sky," Thoreau says,
"Heaven is under our feet as well as over our heads." "A
dark ripple as the wind came creeping," Tennyson uses the
same phenomenon to illustrate the effect of a smile,

> " that like a wrinkling wind
> On glassy water drove his cheek in lines."

"The fishhawks screamed," and "the crows flew," are
special cases under the general statement about the conscious-
ness of all nature. "Clamorously," note the adjective power of
the adverb—not the "flying" but the "crows" were clamorous.

4. "Rolled in volumes," used in reference to the swelling
rounded forms of the clouds. "Summits still bright," why ?
"Bellying," distended. "Rattling," do you think this word
expressive ? "The lightning leaped," Byron phrased it :
"From peak to peak . . leaps the live thunder." "Split-
ting and rending," note the distinction. "Bellow back,"
suggested by the name Bull Hill. Emerson speaks of "the
bellowing of the savage sea."

5. "Scudding rack," broken flying clouds. Longfellow
has "the driving rack of the rain cloud." "Illumined
still more fearfully," made more fearful by being lighted.
"Streams of lightning," in "The Ancient Mariner" Coleridge
wrote "the lightning fell, a river steep and wide."

Washington Irving has been called the literary discoverer of the Hudson; not, I suppose, because upon his soul first dawned the beauty and sublimity of the scenery amid which this noble river flows, but because he first responded to its wonders in perfect literary expression. We are shown some of those beauties in this extract. Elsewhere in his writings Irving has painted pictures of this stream which may well be shown to the class while it is making a study of the above extract. Here are two of them :

a. "The vast bosom of the Hudson was like an unruffled mirror, reflecting the golden splendor of the heavens. . The deceived but delighted eye sought vainly to discern, in the broad masses of shade, the separating line between the land and the water."

b. "He (Rip Van Winkle) saw at a distance the lordly Hudson, far, far below him, moving on its silent but majestic course, with the reflection of a purple cloud, or the sail of a lagging bark here and there sleeping on its glassy bosom, and at last losing itself in the blue highlands."

A picture of the Highlands would be helpful in this connection, and one might be obtained from a Hudson River Railway agent.

THE DEATH OF THE FLOWERS.

1. The melancholy days are come, the saddest of
    the year,
    Of wailing winds, and naked woods, and mead-
    ows brown and sere.
    Heaped in the hollows of the grove, the autumn
    leaves lie dead ;
    They rustle to the eddying gust, and to the rab-
    bit's tread.
    The robin and the wren are flown, and from the
    shrubs the jay,
    And from the wood-top calls the crow through all
    the gloomy day.

2. Where are the flowers, the fair young flowers,
    that lately sprang and stood
  In brighter light and softer airs, a beauteous sis-
    terhood ?
  Alas ! they all are in their graves, the gentle race
    of flowers
  Are lying in their lowly beds, with the fair and
    good of ours.
  The rain is falling where they lie, but the cold
    November rain
  Calls not from out the gloomy earth the lovely
    ones again.

3. The wind-flower and the violet, they perished
    long ago,
  And the brier-rose and the orchis died amid the
    summer glow ;
  But on the hill the golden-rod, and the aster in
    the wood,
  And the yellow sunflower by the brook in
    autumn beauty stood,
  Till fell the frost from the clear cold heaven, as
    falls the plague on men,
  And the brightness of their smile was gone from
    upland, glade, and glen.

4. And now, when comes the calm mild day, as still
    such days will come,
  To call the squirrel and the bee from out their
    winter home ;
  When the sound of dropping nuts is heard,
    though all the trees are still,

And twinkle in the smoky light the waters of the
  rill,
The south-wind searches for the flowers whose
  fragrance late he bore,
And sighs to find them in the wood and by the
  stream no more.

William Cullen Bryant.

1. What makes these days melancholy ? Why is it not
whistling or howling winds ? Where have the robin and the
wren gone ? About what time do they come back ? Does not
the jay in the central states stay all the year ? How about the
crow ? Why do the dead leaves heap in the " hollows " ? Is
the rustle of the dry leaves a melancholy sound to your ear ?

2. Why is the question asked about the flowers ? " Brighter "
than what ? Why called a " sisterhood " ? Why are we told
that the " November " rain does not call out the·flowers ?

3. Notice the use of " they " in the first line of this stanza.
Does golden-rod grow only on hills ? Are all sunflowers
" yellow " ? What is " autumn beauty " ? Does the frost
fall ? How long do the flowers stand in autumn beauty ?

4. How does the mild day call the squirrel and the bee ?
What do they do ? Where is the winter home of the squirrel ?
What " twinkle " ? What is the cause of the twinkling ?
Shakespeare says the sweet south wind breathes upon a bank
of violets, stealing and giving odors : compare this with the
fifth line. Why does the poet call the sound of the wind a
" sigh " ?

TO A WATERFOWL.

1.   Whither, midst falling dew,
    While glow the heavens with the last steps of day,
    Far, through their rosy depths, dost thou pursue
        Thy solitary way ?

2.   Vainly the fowler's eye
Might mark thy distant flight to do thee wrong,
As, darkly seen against the crimson sky,
          Thy figure floats along.

3.   Seek'st thou the plashy brink
Of weedy lake, or marge of river wide,
Or where the rocking billows rise and sink
          On the chafed ocean-side ?

4.   There is a Power whose care
Teaches thy way along that pathless coast—
The desert and illimitable air—
          Lone wandering, but not lost.

5.   All day thy wings have fanned,
At that far height, the cold, thin atmosphere,
Yet stoop not, weary, to the welcome land,
          Though the dark night is near.

6.   And soon that toil shall end ;
Soon shalt thou find a summer home, and rest,
And scream among thy fellows ; reeds shall bend,
          Soon, o'er thy sheltered nest.

7.   Thou'rt gone, the abyss of heaven
Hath swallowed up thy form ; yet on my heart
Deeply has sunk the lesson thou hast given,
          And shall not soon depart.

8.   He who, from zone to zone,
Guides through the boundless sky thy certain flight,
In the long way that I must tread alone,
          Will lead my steps aright.

                                   William Cullen Bryant.

1. If there were no sign at the end of this stanza, how would you know it to be a question? Should it end with the rising inflection? Note the trochees in this stanza. Does dew really fall? Who was midst the dew? Name the two words which suggest the color of the sky. Do they agree? "Rosy .depths." Who were called "Wanderers of the upper deep"? "Last steps," the greatest of poets wrote of morning: "Jocund day stands tiptoe on the misty mountain tops." What does "solitary" add to the picture? Where was this way "pursued"?

2. What "might mark"? Might mark what? Why? How? Why vainly? Why "painted"? Explain use of the word "floats."

3. To what does the poet turn his mind in this stanza? Explain the meaning of "plashy," and "marge." Why do you think the use of the word "chafed" particularly appropriate? Why call billows "rocking"? "Nothing about the sea is more impressive than its ceaseless rocking." —*John Burroughs.*

4. The word "Power," capitalized, means what? "Teaches," points out, guides, directs. Why "pathless coast"? Why "desert"? "illimitable"? What does "wandering" describe? Why is it "not lost"? "Lone wandering," "solitary way."

5. Do you think the use of the word "fanned" descriptive? Why "cold" and "thin"? Is the bird "weary"? the land "welcome"? Why "stoop not"?

6. In what direction was this bird flying? Where would its "summer home be"? In what sort of places does it build its nest? Is the bird "solitary" now?

7. How is "gone" explained in the stanza? Explain "swallowed." Scotland's great poet, describing a storm, says the darkness "swallowed" the gleam of the lightning. "Yet," is this better than "and"? What "shall not soon depart"? Why not? Is "heart" better than "mind"? What is this "lesson"?

8. Can you express this lesson in one word? Do you think

it is Faith ?   Name some points of likeness between the poet
and the bird.

AN OLD-FASHIONED ORCHARD.

1. In these modern days men have lost the pleasures
of the orchard ; yet an old-fashioned orchard is the most
delicious of all places wherein to idle away the after-
noon of a hazy autumn day.

There the sun seems to shine with a soft slumber-
ous warmth without glare, as if the rays came through
an aerial spider's web spun across the sky, letting all
the beauty, but not the heat, slip through its invisible
meshes.

2. There is a shadowy coolness in the recesses
under the trees.

On the damson trunks are yellowish knobs of gum
which has exuded from the bark.

Now and then a leaf rustles to the ground, and at
longer intervals an apple falls with a decided thump.

3. It is silent, save for the gentle twittering of the
swallows on the topmost branches,—they are talking
of their coming journey,—and, perhaps, occasionally
the distant echo of a shot, when the lead has gone
whistling among a covey.

It is a place to dream in, bringing with you a chair
to sit on,—for it will be freer from insects than the
garden-seat,—and a book.

4. Put away all thoughts of time : often in striving
to get the most value from our time it slips from us,
as the reality did from the dog that greedily grasped
at the shadow : simply dream of what you will, with
apples and plums, nuts and filberts within reach.

5. Dusky oranges with a gleam of gold under the

rind ; a warmer tint of yellow on the pippins. Here streaks of red, there a tawny hue, yonder a load of great russets ; near by heavy pears bending the strong branches ; round black damsons ; luscious egg-plums hanging their yellow ovals overhead.

6. On the walnut trees bunches of round green balls : note those that show a dark spot or streak, and gently tap them with the tip of the tall slender pole placed there for the purpose. Down they come glancing from bough to bough, and, striking the hard turf, the thick green rind splits asunder, and the walnut itself rebounds upward.

7. Those who buy walnuts have no idea of the fine taste of the fruit thus gathered direct from the tree.

Surely it is an error to banish the orchard and the fruit-garden from the pleasure-grounds of modern houses, transferring them to the rear, as if something to be ashamed of.

Thomas Hughes.

1. Can you give one reason why men have "lost" these pleasures? What serves as an "aerial web" to entangle the heat?

2. Explain "shadowy coolness." What is that "gum" made of ? "Thump." " In the stillest afternoon, if I listened, the thump of a great apple was audible, falling without a breath of wind, from the mere necessity of perfect ripeness." —*Hawthorne.*

3. Are swallows in this country likely to be seen in groups upon apple trees ? What journey ? Do swallows migrate ? Why the "echo," not the shot itself ? Does the idler in the orchard hear the "whistling" ?

THE CLOSING SCENE.

1. WITHIN his sober realm of leafless trees
   The russet year inhaled the dreamy air ;

Like some tanned reaper in his hour of ease,
When all the fields are lying brown and bare.

2. The gray barns looking from their hazy hills
O'er the dim waters widening in the vales,
Sent down the air a greeting to the mills,
On the dull thunder of alternate flails.

3. All sights were mellowed, and all sounds subdued,
The hills seemed farther, and the streams sang
low ;
As in a dream the distant woodman hewed
His winter log with many a muffled blow.

4. The embattled forests, erewhile armed in gold,
Their banners bright with every martial hue,
Now stood, like some sad beaten host of old,
Withdrawn afar in time's remotest blue.

5. On slumb'rous wings the vulture held his flight ;
The dove scarce heard his sighing mate's com-
plaint ;
And like a star slow drowning in the light,
The village church-vane seemed to pale and
faint.

6. The sentinel cock upon the hillside crew—
Crew thrice, and all was stiller than before,—
Silent till some replying warder blew
His alien horn, and then was heard no more.

7. Where erst the jay, within the elm's tall crest,
Made garrulous trouble round her unfledged
young,
And where the oriole hung her swaying nest,
By every light wind like a censer swung ;—

8. Where sang the noisy masons of the eaves,
    The busy swallows, circling ever near,
Foreboding, as the rustic mind believes,
    An early harvest and a plenteous year ;—

9. Where every bird which charmed the vernal feast,
    Shook the sweet slumber from its wings at morn,
To warn the reaper of the rosy east,—
    All now was songless, empty, and forlorn.

10. Alone from out the stubble piped the quail,
     And croaked the crow through all the dreary
        gloom ;
Alone the pheasant, drumming in the vale,
     Made echo to the distant cottage loom.

11. There was no bud, no bloom upon the bowers ;
     The spiders wove their thin shrouds night by
        night ;
The thistle-down, the only ghost of flowers,
     Sailed slowly by, passed noiseless out of sight.
                    Thomas Buchanan Read.

1. What are compared in this stanza ? Name the points of
likeness.
2. Why is this greeting sent to the *mills* ? " Alternate flails,"
two men handle the flails, and first one and then the other,
strikes the sheaves.

   "And merrily with oft repeated stroke,
    Sounds from the threshing floor the busy flail."
                    —*Longfellow.*
3. Is it the woodman that seemed to dream ?
4. Name the terms suggesting war. How does a hill at a
distance look in Indian summer ? What does " time's remotest
blue " mean ? Explain what " of old " means.

5. "Slumb'rous wings," did you ever see a buzzard soaring? Why is a star said to be "drowning" in the light?

6. Would it really be "stiller than before"? What is the "replying warder," "alien horn." What was "silent"?

7. Does the jay spend the winter in your neighborhood? the oriole? the swallow? What colors has the oriole?

8. Why are swallows called "noisy masons"? "Foreboding"? In what sense is it used here?

9. "To warn the reaper," how? "Rosy east," the coming of morning.

10. Explain "dreary gloom," "echo," "loom."

11. Turn your attention to the sounds of this poem one by one. Listen to them.

THE SNOWSTORM.

1. Through the hushed air the whitening shower descends,
   At first thin wavering ; till at last the flakes
   Fall broad and wide and fast, dimming the day,
   With a continual flow.   The cherished fields
   Put on their winter robe of purest white.
   'Tis brightness all; save where the new snow melts
   Along the mazy current.

2.   Low the woods
   Bow their hoar head ; and, ere the languid sun
   Faint from the west emits his evening ray,
   Earth's universal face, deep hid and chill,
   Is one wild dazzling waste, that buries wide
   The works of man.

3.   Drooping, the laborer-ox
   Stands covered o'er with snow, and then demands
   The fruit of all his toil.   The fowls of heaven,

Tamed by the cruel season, crowd around
The winnowing store, and claim the little boon
Which Providence assigns them.

4.   One alone,
The redbreast, sacred to the household gods,
Wisely regardful of the embroiling sky,
In joyless fields and thorny thickets leaves
His shivering mates, and pays to trusted man
His annual visit.

5.   Half afraid, he first
Against the window beats ; then, brisk, alights
On the warm hearth ; then, hopping o'er the floor,
Eyes all the smiling family askance,
And pecks, and starts, and wonders where he is ;
Till, more familiar grown, the table-crumbs
Attract his slender feet.

6.   The foodless wilds
Pour forth their brown inhabitants.   The hare,
Though timorous of heart, and hard beset
By death in various forms, dark snares and dogs,
And more unpitying man, the garden seeks,
Urged on by fearless want.   The bleating kind
Eye the bleak heaven, and next the glistening
     earth,
With looks of dumb despair ; then, sad dispersed,
Dig for the withered herb through heaps of snow.

7. Now, shepherds, to your helpless charge be kind,
Baffle the raging year, and fill their pens
With food at will ; lodge them below the storm,
And watch them strict ; for from the bellowing
     east,

In this dire season, oft the whirlwind's wing
Sweeps up the burden of whole wintry plains
In one wide waft, and o'er the hapless flocks,
Hid in the hollow of two neighboring hills,
The billowy tempest 'whelms ; till, upward urged,
The valley to a shining mountain swells,
Tipped with a wreath high-curling in the sky.

James Thomson.

(There should be no difficulty with the rhythm of this selection of blank verse—five feet to the line, usually iambics though fourteen lines begin with a trochee. Notice that two consecutive broken lines always, together, make a full line.)

1. "Hushed," the wind does not blow as in Emerson's snow-storm. The snow came gradually, fluctuatingly. "Broad," freely. "As broad and general as the casing air."—*Shakespeare.* "Wide," extensively. "The wounded coveys, reeling, scatter wide."—*Burns.* "New snow," it melts as it falls and does not whiten the crooked brown line. "That great snow never ceased a moment for three days and nights ; and then the topmost hedges were unseen and the trees broke down wherever the wind had not lightened them."—*Black-more.*

2. "Languid sun," poetic for sunset. "Waste." "Old ocean's gray and melancholy waste."—*Bryant.* "Faint," etc. perhaps, as in Whittier's "Snow-bound," "It sank from sight before it set." "The works of man," "A universe of sky and snow."—*Whittier.*

3. "Drooping," with head hanging down. The fowls want a boon, a *gift ;* while the ox demands his *pay.*

4. "The redbreast," dear to the household gods, the divinities that preside over homes, for its service in the little tragedy of the Babes in the Woods.

5. A beautiful and true picture. Can you verify it from your experience ? Does our redbreast hop ? walk ? run ?

6. "The hare." Note the following quotation from Blackmore. "Before half the frost was over, all we had in the snowy ditches were hares so tame that you could pat them." "Hard beset," in danger of his life. "Dark snares," hidden traps. "Fearless, "hunger makes him bold. "Kind," family. "Bleating kind," sheep. "Glistening," white, covered with snow.

> "Around the glistening wonder bent
> The blue walls of the firmament."—*Whittier.*

7. After describing the storm, the landscape, the behavior of certain animals, the poet appeals to pity in the hearts of the shepherds. "Charge," the animals given into the shepherd's care. "Baffle," defeat the attacks of. "Burden," the great mass of snow. "Waft," sweep. "With one waft of the wing."—*Tennyson.*

"There was no flock at all to be seen ; only at one corner of the field, by the eastern end, where the snow drove in, a great white billow, as high as a barn and as broad as a house. This great drift was rolling and curling beneath the violent blast, and all the while from the smothering sky, came the pelting, pitiless arrows, winged with murky white, and pointed with the barbs of frost."—*Blackmore.*

ELEGY WRITTEN IN A COUNTRY CHURCHYARD.

1. THE curfew tolls the knell of parting day,
    The lowing herd wind slowly o'er the lea,
 The plowman homeward plods his weary way,
    And leaves the world to darkness and to me.

2. Now fades the glimmering landscape on the sight,
    And all the air a solemn stillness holds,
 Save where the beetle wheels his droning flight,
    And drowsy tinklings lull the distant folds ;

Read. and Comp.—10.

3. Save that from yonder ivy-mantled tower
    The moping owl does to the moon complain
Of such as, wand'ring near her secret bower,
    Molest her ancient solitary reign.

4. Beneath those rugged elms, that yew tree's shade,
    Where heaves the turf in many a mold'ring
      heap,
Each in his narrow cell forever laid,
    The rude Forefathers of the hamlet sleep.

5. The breezy call of incense-breathing Morn,
    The swallow twitt'ring from the straw-built
      shed,
The cock's shrill clarion, or the echoing horn,
    No more shall rouse them from their lowly bed.

6. For them no more the blazing hearth shall burn,
    Or busy housewife ply her evening care;
No children run to lisp their sire's return,
    Or climb his knees the envied kiss to share.

7. Oft did the harvest to their sickle yield,
    Their furrow oft the stubborn glebe has broke;
How jocund did they drive their team afield!
    How bowed the woods beneath their sturdy
      stroke!

8. Let not Ambition mock their useful toil,
    Their homely joys, and destiny obscure;
Nor Grandeur hear, with a disdainful smile,
    The short and simple annals of the poor.

9. The boast of heraldry, the pomp of power,
    And all that beauty, all that wealth e'er gave,
Awaits alike, th' inevitable hour.
    The paths of glory lead but to the grave.

10. Nor you, ye Proud, impute to these the fault,
    If Mem'ry o'er their tomb no trophies raise,
    Where through the long-drawn aisle and fretted
        vault
    The pealing anthem swells the note of praise.

11. Can storied urn or animated bust
    Back to its mansion call the fleeting breath ?
    Can Honor's voice provoke the silent dust,
    Or Flatt'ry soothe the dull, cold ear of Death ?

12· Perhaps in this neglected spot is laid
    Some heart once pregnant with celestial fire ;
    Hands that the rod of empire might have swayed,
    Or waked to ecstasy the living lyre.

13. But Knowledge to their eyes her ample page,
    Rich with the spoils of time, did ne'er unroll :
    Chill Penury repress'd their noble rage,
    And froze the genial current of the soul.

14. Full many a gem of purest ray serene
    The dark unfathomed caves of ocean bear ;
    Full many a flower is born to blush unseen,
    And waste its sweetness on the desert air.

15. Some village Hampden, that with dauntless breast
    The little tyrant of his fields withstood ;
    Some mute inglorious Milton here may rest,
    Some Cromwell guiltless of his country's blood.

16. Th' applause of list'ning senates to command,
    The threats of pain and ruin to despise,
    To scatter plenty o'er a smiling land,
    And read their history in a nation's eyes,

17. Their lot forbade ; nor circumscribed alone
     Their growing virtues, but their crimes confined ;
   Forbade to wade through slaughter to a throne,
     And shut the gates of mercy on mankind,

18. The struggling pangs of conscious truth to hide,
     To quench the blushes of ingenuous shame,
   Or heap the shrine of Luxury and Pride
     With incense kindled at the Muse's flame.

19. Far from the madding crowd's ignoble strife,
     Their sober wishes never learned to stray ;
   Along the cool sequestered vale of life,
     They kept the noiseless tenor of their way.

20. Yet ev'n these bones from insult to protect
     Some frail memorial still erected nigh,
   With uncouth rimes and shapeless sculpture
       decked,
     Implores the passing tribute of a sigh.

21. Their name, their years, spelled by th' unletter'd
       Muse,
     The place of fame and elegy supply ;
   And many a holy text around she strews,
     That teach the rustic moralist to die.

22. For who, to dumb Forgetfulness a prey,
     This pleasing anxious being e'er resigned,
   Left the warm precincts of the cheerful day,
     Nor cast one longing, ling'ring look behind ?

23. On some fond breast the parting soul relies,
     Some pious drops the closing eye requires ;
   Ev'n from the tomb the voice of Nature cries,
     Ev'n in our ashes live their wonted fires.

24. For thee, who mindful of th' unhonored Dead
    Dost in these lines their artless tale relate,
If chance, by lonely contemplation led,
    Some kindred spirit shall inquire thy fate,

25. Haply some hoary-headed swain may say,
    "Oft have we seen him at the peep of dawn
Brushing with hasty steps the dews away
    To meet the sun upon the upland lawn.

26. " There at the foot of yonder nodding beech,
    That wreathes its old fantastic roots so high,
His listless length at noontide would he stretch,
    And pore upon the brook that babbles by.

27. " Hard by yon wood, now smiling as in scorn,
    Mutt'ring his wayward fancies he would rove ;
Now drooping, woeful wan, like one forlorn,
    Or crazed with care, or crossed in hopeless love.

28. " One morn I missed him from the custom'd hill,
    Along the heath and near his fav'rite tree ;
Another came ; nor yet beside the rill,
    Nor up the lawn, nor at the wood was he ;

29. "The next with dirges due in sad array
    Slow through the churchway path we saw him
       borne,
Approach and read (for thou canst read) the lay,
    Graved on the stone beneath yon agèd thorn."

THE EPITAPH.

30. *Here rests his head upon the lap of Earth*
    A Youth, to Fortune and to Fame unknown.
Fair Science frowned not on his humble birth,
    And Melancholy marked him for her own.

31. *Large was his bounty, and his soul sincere,*
Heav'n did a recompense as largely send;
He gave to Misery all he had, a tear,
He gained from Heav'n ('twas all he wished) a
friend.

32. *No farther seek his merits to disclose,*
Or draw his frailties from their dread abode,
(There they alike in trembling hope repose,)
The bosom of his Father and his God.

Thomas Gray.

Thomas Gray, the famous English poet, was born in Corn-hill, London, December 26, 1716.

In 1727 he went to Eton College and afterwards to Cambridge University, which he left in 1738 without taking his degree. After a tour on the continent in company with Horace Walpole, he returned to England and took up his residence at Cambridge.

Although one of the finest scholars of his time, he wrote but little, owing to his reserve, his critical temper, and his horror of publicity. His famous Elegy, published in 1751, placed him in the front rank of English poets.

Gray died in 1771, and is buried in the little churchyard of Stoke Pogis, which is supposed to be the one immortalized in his poem.

"Had Gray written nothing but his 'Elegy,' high as he stands, I am not sure that he would not stand higher."—*Byron.*

"Had Gray written often thus," (as in some of the finer stanzas of the 'Elegy') "it had been vain to blame, and useless to praise him."—*Samuel Johnson.*

1. The story of the curfew should be read in English history. Day is dying and its knell is sounded from the tower of the little church. While listening to the bell, the poet sees the cattle following the winding path across the meadow, and he notes the plowman trudging homeward.

2. Note " glimmering." " The west yet glimmers with some streaks of day."—*Shakespeare*. Stillness charms the air and there is no sound, except the droning, or humming, of the beetle and the tinkling of cow bells. Why "drowsy"?

> " Or where the beetle winds
>   His small but sullen horn."
>
> —*Collins.*

Read this second stanza, omitting the words "glimmering," "solemn," "droning," "drowsy," and notice how faded a picture is left.

3. "Ivy-mantled" conveys what impression?   What is the meaning of "bower" here?   "Ancient," for many years the owl has nested there alone.

4. "Elms," "yew tree's shade," the interlacing branches form a canopy over the graves, as a "low green tent whose curtain never outward swings."—*Whittier.*

5. The moist air of the morning or evening carries the odor of flower and shrub.

> " But now the gentle dew-fall sends abroad
>   The fruit-like perfume of the golden furze."
>
> —*Coleridge.*

"Shrill clarion," "The cock that is the trumpet to the morn."—*Shakespeare*. Neither the stir of the breeze, the crowing of the cock, nor the blast of the horn shall ever again rouse them from their humble couches to duty.

6. "Evening care," what do you think it was?

7. Here we have a partial list of a farmer's tasks. "Glebe," what is it?   Why "stubborn"?

8. What is meant by "Ambition" and "Grandeur"?   Can you explain the reason for this personification?

9. High birth, office, beauty, riches, for each of these the *hour* waits.

10. "Trophies," no stately stones are erected over these humble graves. What sort of a burial service do lines three and four suggest?

11. "Storied urn," a funeral urn engraved with the deeds of the dead. Hawthorne calls Trajan's column a "storied shaft," Milton speaks of a "storied window," Tennyson points to "snowy summits old in story." "Provoke," call forth the dead to life. "Dull cold ear," what makes these words peculiarly descriptive here?

> " And when I am forgotten, as I shall be,
>   And sleep in dull, cold marble."
>   —*Shakespeare.*

12. "Pregnant," stirred by the divinity of genius. "Rod," scepter, the symbol of power. "Lyre," the muse of poetry.

13. "Spoils," accumulated learning. "Chill Penury" checked their enthusiasm, cooled their warm impulses.

14. Compare with this stanza the following from Emerson :

> "Rhodora ! if the sages ask thee why
>   This charm is wasted on the earth and sky,
>   Tell them, dear, that if eyes were made for seeing,
>   Then Beauty is its own excuse for being."

"Serene," fair. "Unfathomed," unmeasured. "Desert," empty.

15. "Hampden," an eminent English statesman who refused to pay the tax of ship-money imposed by Charles I. As the rustic patriot was a "village Hampden," so his oppressor was a "little tyrant," a village Charles. What do you think was Gray's opinion of Milton? of Cromwell? In the original manuscript of this poem the characters used for illustration were Cato, Tully (Cicero), and Cæsar, instead of Hampden, Milton, and Cromwell. English literature has learned slowly that it can stay at home.

16, 17, 18. Their humble station prevented them from swaying audiences by their eloquence, from causing a whole land to smile with plenty, and from reading the effects of their good deeds in the loving eyes of their countrymen.   But, on the other hand, it forbade them to play the tyrant, to gratify their ambition by the death of the innocent, to stifle conscience, and to flatter the proud and luxurious.

19. Living "far from" . . . , their sober wishes did not stray   "Madding," the more correct form would be "maddening."

20. "Yet," see the tenth stanza.   "Shapeless sculpture," rude carving.   "In Gray's Elegy is there an image more striking than his 'shapeless sculpture' ? "—*Byron.*

21. "Unletter'd Muse," some village poet.   To spell the name and age of "the poor inhabitant below" would not call for much help from the Muse, nor even to copy the Scripture verse which may help him who reads to look upon death less fearfully, a help sorely needed.

22. Who ever gave up this life of mingled joy and sorrow without looking back longingly, lingeringly ?

23. "Parting soul," dying person.   "Pious drops," tears of sympathy.

24. Note the syntax of "thee."   Compare it with Webster's "him whose honored name the gentleman himself bears
does he suppose me less capable," etc., and with Stoddard's

> "Me whom the city holds, whose feet
>   Have worn its stony highways,
> Familiar with its loneliest street,
>   Its ways were never my ways."

25. "Hoary-headed swain," gray-haired rustic.   "Lawn," an open space in the woods.   After stanza 25, the original manuscript had the following :

> " Him have we seen the greenwood side along,
>   While o'er the heath we hied, our labors done;
> Oft as the woodlark piped her farewell song,
>   With wistful eyes pursue the setting sun."

26. "Fantastic roots," see "As You Like It," Act II., Sc. 1. The melancholy Jacques mourned over the sad fate of the stricken deer as he lay

> " Under an oak, whose antique root peeps out."

"Babbles," brawls, murmurs, sings. What other names do poets apply to the brook's music?

27. "Woeful wan," do these words intensify the description of his sadness ?

28. "Customed hill," the upland lawn.

> " And from the breathing lawn a forest springs." —*Shelley*.

"The heath," named in the omitted stanza above. "Favorite tree," the nodding beech. Gray liked this word : " Beyond the meadow nods a thicket of oaks."

29. "Dirges," funeral hymns. "Sad array,"—"suits of solemn black."—"Hamlet," Act I., Sc. 2. "For thou canst read," which the hoary-headed swain could not do. In one manuscript, Gray had inserted, after this stanza, the following:

> There scattered oft, the earliest of the year,
>   By hands unseen, are showers of violets found;
> The redbreast loves to build, and warble there,
>   And little footsteps lightly print the ground.

"Scattered," by unseen hands. By whom are these "showers of violets" found ? Does the "redbreast" build in the thorn ? Whose footsteps "lightly print the ground" ?

30. Note the expression "lap of Earth." What does it mean? "Science," knowledge. "Melancholy," meditation.

> " Ye brown o'erarching groves,
>   That Contemplation loves,
> Where willowy Camus lingers with delight!
>   Oft at the blush of dawn
>   I trod your level lawn,

Oft wooed the gleam of Cynthia silver-bright
In cloisters dim, far from the haunts of Folly,
With Freedom by my side, and soft-eyed Melancholy."
                            —*Gray's* " Ode for Music."

31. " Bounty," liberality.   " Recompense," reward.

32. His good traits and his evil ones are fully known to God alone.

" Then with my good and ill unreckoned,
    And both forgiven by Thine abounding grace."
                                        —*Whittier.*

INDEX.

Accent, often determined by the rhythm, 27, 28.
Addison, Joseph, *The Spacious Firmament on High*, 99.
Aftermath, definition of, 71.
Analysis, 11.
Anapest, 25.
An Old-Fashioned Orchard, Thomas Hughes, 138.
April Weather, Celia Thaxter, 91.
Authors quoted in the notes: Bible, 98; Blackmore, 144, 145; Bolles, 121; Bryant, 114, 117, 129, 144; Burns, 144; Burroughs, 104, 137; Byron, 132, 153; Coleridge, 132, 151; Collins, 151; Emerson, 123, 132, 152; Goldsmith, 124, 131; Gray, 155; Hawthorne, 139, 152; Irving, 133; Johnson, 150; Keyser, 123; Kingsley, 90; Longfellow, 128, 132, 141; Lowell, 91; Milton, 90, 124, 131,152; Shakespeare, 100, 108, 114, 131, 135, 137, 144, 151, 152, 154; Shelley, 104, 123, 154; Stoddard, 153; Tennyson, 123, 132, 145, 152; Thoreau, 132; Webster, 153; Whittier, 144, 145, 151, 155.

Birds mentioned in the notes: Bee-martin, 49; Blackbird, English, 90; Bluebird, 60; Buzzard, 142; Chickadee, 123; Cock, 151; Crow, 132; Crow blackbirds, 108; Dove, 69; Eagle, 67, 132; Fish-hawk, 132; Flycatcher, 49; Goldfinch, 48, 108; Grackles, 108; Jay, 108, 135, 142; Kingbird, 49; Kinglet, 123; Lark, 90, 116, 117, 123, 124, 126 : Nightingale, 90; Oriole, 105, 142; Owl, 151; Redbreast, 154; Robin, 48, 60, 104, 135; Rook, 108; Song Sparrow, 48; Swallow, 60, 72, 105; Waterfowl, 137; Wren, 105, 135; Yellow Warbler, 108..
Blank verse, turning prose into, 29.
Boyle, Margaret P., *How the Horse-Chestnut Got its Name*, 72.
Brandywine Ford, Bayard Taylor, 79.
Bryant, William Cullen, *The Death of the Flowers*, 133; *The Gladness of Nature*, 104; *To a Waterfowl*, 135; *To the Fringed Gentian*, 78.
Burns, Robert, *To A Mountain Daisy*, 114.
Burritt, Elihu, *The English Skylark*, 122.

Cary, Alice, *Pretty is That Pretty Does*, 56; *What a Bird Taught*, 47.
Cesura, 27.
Cesural pause, 25, note.
Composition, oral, 43; specimen outlines for, 44, 45.
Cornucopia, 113.
Criticism, elementary, 21, 22.
Curfew, 151.

Dactyl, 25, 27.

157

Pretty is That Pretty Does, Alice Cary, 56.

Prose, for memorizing, 39–42.

Prosody, boy's definition of, 25.

Rattle of bars, 122.

Read, Thomas Buchanan, *The Closing Scene*, 139 ; *The Rising*, 98.

Reading, art of, neglected, 12, 13, 15 ; oral, exercises in, 19, 20 ; time spent in, 17, 18.

Rhythm, 25–32 ; exercises in, 29, 30 ; in *Lorna Doone*, 31.

Roberts, Sarah, *The Voice of the Grass*, 64.

September, Helen Hunt Jackson, 62.

Shillalah, mentioned by Lowell, 34.

Some of Lowell's Garden Acquaintances, James Russell Lowell, 106.

Sounds of nature in a poem, 75, 105.

Spider, 56.

Spondee, 25, 27.

Strawberries, J. T. Trowbridge, 59.

Study, course of, 17.

Style, elements of, 21–24.

Taylor, Bayard, *Brandywine Ford*, 79.

Thaxter, Celia, *April Weather*, 91 ; *The Sandpiper*, 96.

The Beaver, 50.

The Children's Flower, 53.

The Closing Scene, Thomas Buchanan Read, 139.

The Concord, Nathaniel Hawthorne, 94.

The Corn Song, John Greenleaf Whitter, 111.

The Death of the Flowers, William Cullen Bryant, 133.

The English Skylark, Elihu Burritt, 122.

The Fiftieth Birthday of Agassiz, Henry Wadsworth Longfellow, 100.

The Fox and the Ducks, 60.

The Gladness of Nature, Wllliam Cullen Bryant, 104.

The Huskers, John Greenleaf Whittier, 109.

The Kaatskills, Washington Irving, 126.

The Kingbird, 48.

The Landing of the Pilgrim Fathers, Mrs. Hemans, 74.

The Lark, John Milton, 117.

The Mountain and the Squirrel, Ralph Waldo Emerson, 101.

The Old Eagle Tree, Dr. John Todd, 65.

The Rainbow, William Wordsworth, 92.

The Raindrop, Mary R. M. Harbison, 118.

The Rising, Thomas Buchanan Read, 98.

The Sandpiper, Celia Thaxter, 96.

The Snowstorm, Ralph Waldo Emerson, 125.

The Snowstorm, James Thomson, 142.

The Spacious Firmament on High, Joseph Addison, 99.

The Squirrel's Arithmetic, 63.

The Swallow's Nest, 71.

The Thunderstorm, Washington Irving, 129.

The Voice of the Grass, Sarah Roberts, 64.

Thomson, James, *The Snowstorm*, 142.

To A Mountain Daisy, Robert Burns, 114.

To a Skylark, William Wordsworth, 124.

To a Waterfowl, William Cullen Bryant, 135.

Todd, Dr. John, *The Old Eagle Tree*, 65.

To the Daisy, William Wordsworth, 117.

To the Dandelion, James Russell Lowell, 102.

To the Fringed Gentian, William Cullen Bryant, 78.

Trochee, 25, 137.

Trowbridge, J. T., *Strawberries*, 59.